By the Same Author

a) **Leadership books**
- *Effective Leadership: The African Challenge*
- *The leader, Five Leader Types*
- *Le leadership Africain : Etats des Lieux Et Perspectives*
- *Integrity: The Key To Durable Success*
- *Created For A Purpose*
- *Quel Avenir Pour Un Leadership Africain?*

b) **Marriage books**
- *Secrets of a Successful Marriage*
- *Family Foundations: Breaking Generational Curses and Building Positive Family Foundations*
- *Premarital Counseling in Seven Steps*
- *Singles and Love Affairs*
- *Making the Right Choice of a Marriage Partner*

c) **Others**
- *The Cross, a Message of Victory to Every Believer*
- *Growing in Your Christian Life*
- *Stop, Reflect on Your Life*

Readers' Comments

I read one of your books entitled, « From Adolescence To Marriage ». This book has greatly helped me in the areas it has handled. I am a young girl 31 of age who is still waiting for God's choice for my life. At age 16, I took a vow before God not to contaminate myself sexually before my marriage and I thank God for having kept that vow till today. Obviously I have faced lots of challenges and had lots of questions whose answers I found in your book which is also mine now. That is why I really want to encourage you in the writing ministry. **S.T.E Burkina Faso**

I thank God for you. I was so touched when I read your book 'From Adolescence To Marriage'. I am a graduate from the university seeking for a job and besides asking the LORD for a life partner. I have learnt a lot from your book and don't want to go astray; please daddy can you help me to pray? Thanks; I will always like to keep in touch with you. **S. N. Cameroon**

I have just read through your book titled FROM ADOLESCENCE TO MARRIAGE. It has marked me so much so that my conscience will not leave if I do not do justice by thanking God for you. I have read so many books on marriage, but none of the books have touched me like this one. **J.M Cameroon**

Thank you for your book "Adolescence to Marriage". I was privileged to have come across it. I pray that you will remain greatly blessed for touching the life of millions across the globe... May the Lord continue to bless you with wisdom and understanding so that you will be an asset to the younger generation, In Jesus Name. **S.B. Cameroon**

I am a born again Christian, I read through your book "From adolescence to marriage". I am engaged with a brother in Full Gospel, I wish to know the importance of honeymoon in the life of a couple. Is there any appropriate time for it? ... Since I gave my life to Christ, I have been listening to your messages and I know you are the right person. Your book "From adolescence to marriage" is leading me in my courtship and all the community where I find myself is really blessed. God Bless. **L.T. Cameroon**

FROM ADOLESCENCE TO MARRIAGE

Scripture quotations except otherwise stated are taken from New International Version (NIV). Other quotations as indicated may be from King James Version (KJV), Revised Standard Version (RSV), and New King James Version (NKJV).

All the names and certain details of case studies mentioned in this book have been changed to protect the privacy of the individuals involved. Our intermittent use of the masculine or feminine gender is not a bias but just a choice of one of the genders in each case and it as well applies to the other.

Daniel Shu

FROM ADOLESCENCE TO MARRIAGE

Making the Right Choice of a Life Partner

Second Edition
Revised and updated

MAP
Kansas City (MO)

From Adolescence To Marriage
Making the Right Choice of A Life Partner

Daniel Shu

Published by
Miraclaire Academic Publications (MAP)
Kansas City, MO 64138, USA

ISBN-13: 978-0615927480 / ISBN-10: 0615927483

MAP is an imprint of Miraclaire Publishing LLC
www.miraclairepublishing.com

Printed in the United States of America

PREFACE

Counseling singles and couples constitutes a major part of our work, my wife and I have organized and participated in many seminars across Africa in the past fifteen years. Through our effort, we have seen marriages transformed into happy unions. Several youths who are happily married today attest that our seminars and/or the first edition of this book impacted on their lives positively. In fact a medical doctor, who is happily married today, came to our home to appreciate us for the seminar we held with in the medical school while he was a student. "Thank you for letting me take the Joseph's vow of chastity in the second year of my medical studies. I received deliverance from promiscuity and each time I was tempted, I held firm to the vow and by His grace I kept myself pure till my marriage."

This book is the outcome of the teachings and interactions from these seminars. It meets the needs of the teenagers who are preparing to get into marriage. I also want to affirm that the ministry to singles is a divinely ordained ministry. When we started our marriage ministry more than twenty years ago, it was specifically for couples. Then after sometime, the Lord began to speak to me. "You are a medical doctor but you are not applying your medical knowledge in your ministry. In medical practice, there is preventive and curative medicine. In preventive medical practice, you learn how to proactively prevent diseases, epidemics, and pandemics. However, in your ministry you have only carried out curative family therapy. You wait for the people to get married and have marital crises and then you step in to resolve. Why don't you practice preventive therapy where you prepare the singles on how to pick up the right partners, prepare for marriage and start, and live their marital lives happily? That is what you should also do. Practice both preventive and curative marriage therapies." In addition, that ushered us into this dimension of our marriage ministry. Today the ministry has four main aspects;

Singles seminars: The unmarried are taught what it takes to prepare for a divinely appointed, honeymoon marriage and make it through life happily as a prophetic couple.

Marriage seminars: These seminars bring together couples who are taught, counseled, and prayed for. We have seen many marriages restored, healed, and revived.

Marriage foundational seminars: In these seminars we show how family foundations can have positive or negative impacts in couples and descendants. These seminars are usually deliverance oriented because many couples and families suffering from foundational links are prayed for and spiritual chains and curses are broken in the name of Jesus.

Counselors training seminars: Both at seminars and in a first degree university program we train marriage counselors. We intend to register a marriage counselor's association that will enable these trained counselors to practice professionally as in the developed world. To our knowledge, this is not yet a practice in the African world.

This volume in your hands is the second updated edition of the book that was published in 2002. We have revised most of the content added lots of contemporary testimonies. It is a worth reading even by those who read the first edition.

Choosing the right lifetime mate is not as easy as ordering a readymade meal from a MacDonald restaurant or settling for roasted chicken. It is a hard decision that entails much consideration. Unfortunately, many youths are often unaware of what to look for and how to differentiate the good from the best. Others become too picky that they miss the best and settle on the undesirable. As we go around holding singles seminars, we have witnessed these situations repeatedly.

Youngsters are often plagued with the following; questions; how do I know if he/she is the right partner? Where is the place to meet the right partner, in the church, youth gatherings, school, pop or anywhere? What are the predispositions for me to meet the right person? How do you start such a relationship? Pastor; help me, how can I know? In one case, a sister confided to me; *"Pastor I like him but I do not really know if I love him. He keeps hovering around me and though there is a negative impulse in me, I am afraid to miss God's choice for my life. He looks handsome and elegant, but his spiritual life is really wanting. I am afraid to miss him and then stay unmarried. I am getting close to X years and I am afraid I am getting too old. Pastor can I just accept and marry him? Pastor, help me please. What should I do?"* This book is meant to help every young person to know how to make the best choice and groom that choice into a vital marriage.

In this volume, you will be informed, reformed and transformed by nuggets you might have never been close to. The risks of adolescent marriages, the precautions needed in making the right choice, the sex dilemma among youths, the differences between lust and love, dating, and courtship, first weeks of marriage and similar topics are part of the gorgeous menu. 'Prevention is better than cure', says a famous dictum. I would add that precaution is an indispensable virtue for those who intend to get married. This book will help you avoid all headaches and heartaches in later life.

After one of our single's seminar with university students, a married computer scientist made this comment to the singles,

"You are fortunate to learn these things before stepping into marriage. We never had such opportunity. We jumped into it completely ignorant of what it entailed. Nobody taught or counselled us. We did not have any guiding books with a local touch to read. We were naïve, needy and neurotic. Thank God, you have all it takes now to be better prepared, seminars, audio and video messages, books and counsellors. You have no reason to fail."

You might never have the opportunity to attend any of our seminars. This book in your hand is more than a seminar. You will have it as a constant reference to guide you on the path of making the right choice. Read it, live it and become a model of a successful youth in his/her marriage.

I want to end with the words of one of some of the wisest men that ever lived on this planet earth,

"Preserve sound judgement and discernment, do not let them out of your sight; they will be life for you, an ornament to grace your neck. Then you will go on your way in safety, and your foot will not stumble; when you lie down, you will not be afraid; when you lie down, your sleep will be sweet" (King Solomon)[1]

Happy reading and welcome to a transformed life experience and testimony! Digest this nuptial preparatory menu for a matrimonial paradise. Enjoy.

---

[1] Proverbs 3:21-24

Contents

CHAPTER 1
Don't Fall Into the Same Pit

Mr. Francis and Grace have been married for fourteen years and have two children. They are both good looking, well-educated and have well-paid jobs. I visited them recently in their magnificent story building only to find out that Grace was no longer leaving at home. They have been separated for the past two years and are in the process of divorce. Each of them is very bitter against the other. For Grace, it has been rough from the very beginning. I ran into her a few weeks at her jobsite, as we were chatting casual, she confided in me.

"Francis is hard and merciless. He has no milk of human kindness or consideration. He is a terror to the children and me. When something annoys him, he looks for the scapegoat on whom to vent his anger and that is me."

She then paused to check the tears that were already collecting in her eyes. Then, she looked at me with misery, wondering what my reaction would be since Francis was a friend of mine. I nodded, encouraging her to continue. She drew closer and in a softer tone added,

"I have borne these torments for all these years thinking that things would change, but things rather deteriorate. The last blow came when I almost lost my life because of his sadistic beating. He even thrust me down the concrete staircase of our home. I barely escaped a vertebral colon fracture. I am done with him. I prefer to live alone and have my life."

I composed myself when I met Francis. I have learnt never to judge until I have heard from both parties. Francis was did not maltreat Grace. According to him, Grace is irresponsible, lazy, and talkative. She cannot take care of their children, their home, or their property. She is a disorganized misfit and he regrets having chosen such an irresponsible woman for a wife. On request to know why they should settle on such a disgraceful separation after so many years of marriage, he responded,

"I could never imagine that it would come to this stage. I kept hoping that she would learn from her mistakes but she seems to be so dull that she cannot learn a thing. I am sorry I often had to use my fist, but I considered it severe correction enough for her to change, but Daniel understand that I am fed up with such a life. It cannot continue any longer. It is time to turn a new page."

*****

I am saddened for Francis and Grace because they are good family friends. Unfortunately, many families are facing this situation be they pagans, professing Christians, or real born-again believers.

I recently talked to a Christian in one of the most industrialized nations of the world.

"Nick, I hear the divorce rate in this nation is very high, one marriage in three; am I right?"

"You are very generous, Daniel." He said. "Actually the current rate is one in two, and not just out there in the world; even in the church."

I looked at him in surprise, wondering whether this was not an exaggeration. Nick, seeing the astonishment on my face, he continued:

"For two years, I have been the leader of the singles in my church, and half of the people in this group, especially the women are divorcees."

Marriage, as an institution, faces more setbacks apart from divorce. Recent American statistics reveal that both the rate of marriages and divorce are dropping while the population is increasing. [2] Marriages the world over are attacked by several factors. As of May 2013, thirteen nations including South Africa (the only African nation) have legalized same sex marriages. Pornography, single parenting, and promiscuity are additional marital plagues of our time.

Adolescent marriages escalate the high rates of divorces, as these couples are often unprepared. According to the Center for Disease Control, National Survey of Family Growth USA

[2] http://www.patheos.com/blogs/blackwhiteandgray/2012/05/marriage-and-divorce-statistics/
Consulted 17th July 2013

the divorce rate is very high for couples under 24 years as shown in the table below[3]

Table 1.1: Percent of Divorces by Age		
Age	Women	Men
Under 20 years old	27.6%	11.7%
20 to 24 years old	36.6%	38.8%
25 to 29 years old	16.4%	22.3%
30 to 34 years old	8.5%	11.6%
35 to 39 years old	5.1%	6.5%

Similarly, below are results of a study carried out in a developing world setting among students concerning virginity. One hundred and forty eight secondary and high school students between the ages of fourteen, and twenty answered a questionnaire and below were the alarming results.

Table 1.2: Youth and sexual habits

Factor studied	Boys %	Girls %	Total %
1. Lost virginity	72	56	63.5
2. Raped	2.9	13	8.7
3. Masturbate	36.7	26	31
4. Aborted	-	2.5	2.5
5. Divorced parents	19	21	20

From the table we realize that 64 percent of our youth lose their virginity before age twenty, close to 9 percent are raped and 31 percent masturbate. That is very serious.

These findings are a pointer to the vulnerability of our youths and their unpreparedness for marriage. There is every reason to understand why many marriages fail, why many do not enjoy their marriages. Most youths see marriage as a nightmarish condition that leads to unhappiness and dashed hopes. These and other interrogations thump the minds of prospective spouses. Our intention is to help prospective candidates find true happiness. Marriage is supposed to be the

---

[3] Centre for Disease Control, National Survey of Family Growth Date Verified: 7.11.2012 http://www.statisticbrain.com/u-s-divorce-rate-statistics/ Consulted 17 July 2013

best relationship on earth after one's commitment to Christ. However, because of ignorance, misunderstanding, and inexperience, many people fall prey to incompatible marital bondages. I pray this would not be your case in JESUS NAME.

You know, in many cases, man struggles to resolve problems only after crises occur. That is often the case in marriage. Many people have not learned to look before leaping. They only see the bright side of marriage; may be sex, enjoyment, companionship, and fulfillment, but they forget that it is also responsibility, effort, problem solving, and a learning process. Many therefore get into it and sooner or later get trapped by the very circumstances they neglected. They then reactively struggle to solve the problems as they occur in the home. There is a better way to go about it. It is the preventive method. Instead of waiting to fall into the trap of a troublesome marriage, it is better to learn from the errors others have made in the past in order to avoid them in your marriage. Then you would set a platform for success. Does not an English dictum say, "Prevention is better than cure?" We learn from past events in history in order to ameliorate the future. Even the Bible tells us that the experiences of others are a lesson for us so that we should not fall into the same errors.

> *Now these things occurred as examples to keep us from setting our hearts on evil things as they did....These things happened to them as examples and were written down as warnings for us, on whom the fulfillment of the ages has come (1 Corinthians 10:6, 11).*

That is the object of this book. Every unmarried or prospective spouse should learn from the experiences of others in order to be better prepared. As you read the remaining chapters, your mind is enriched with the knowledge *of who you are, what you can do to improve your personality and how to make the right choice of a life partner, God being your guide.* You should be a success and not a failure. Let your future marriage and home become the best that God ever meant it to be. Let this be said of you as King Solomon wrote that:

"My lover is mine and I am his...
And his banner over me is love." (SS 2: 4, 16)

CHAPTER 2
Introduction to temperaments

The problems of Francis and Grace are very common in many marriages in our society. Even when couples stay under the same roof and drive in the same car, you would be surprised that some sleep in separate rooms, others do not speak to each other and others are barely managing to put up appearances. Not a great percentage of couples really enjoy the marriage life. Our desire is that you who are planning to get married would experience fulfillment in your matrimonial home as God intended. One of the major problems we have observed is personality conflict. This is the major problem of Francis and Grace. In this chapter, we want you to discover your personality in order to develop your strengths and work on your weaknesses before marriage so that they do not become an obstacle in your relationship with your spouse.

Understanding your personality
     I want to introduce you to '**who you are**' and that is your personality or better still your temperament. Temperament is a person's disposition or nature that affects his ways of thinking, feeling, and behavior. All of us have inherited a basic temperament from our parents, which reveals in our strengths and weaknesses. Information inherited from parents is coded on genes and is called the **genotype**. Our genotype is responsible for our natural temperament. In addition, another element influences character formation- the environment in which we grow. Our personality is shaped enormously by these two elements represented as follows:

Genotype + Environmental Influence = Natural Character
(Temperament)   (Environment)   (Natural personality)
(Nature)   (Nurture)   (Norm)

The above equation depicts the unsaved or those who are still ignorant of the ways of Christ. When one accepts Jesus Christ as Savior and Lord, another important element comes to the character molding process, and that is the Holy Spirit. He begins to work deep within us, not to change our genotype, but to influence through the environment, our character. Thus for believers the equation is modified as follows:

Genotype + Environment + Holy Spirit = Transformed Character
(Temperament) (Natural) (Divine) (Spiritual Man)

That is why the Bible says in Romans 12: 1-2, *"Therefore, I urge you, brothers, in view of God's mercy, to offer your bodies as living sacrifices, holy and pleasing to God-- this is your spiritual act of worship. Do not conform any longer to the pattern of this world, but be transformed by the renewing of your mind. Then you will be able to test and approve what God's will is-- his good, pleasing and perfect will"*.

Man is a spirit that lives in a body controlled by his soul. Transformation takes place at the level of the soul that influences the body. We can illustrate this truth of Scripture in the following diagram:

Fig 2.1: The human being –Trichotomy

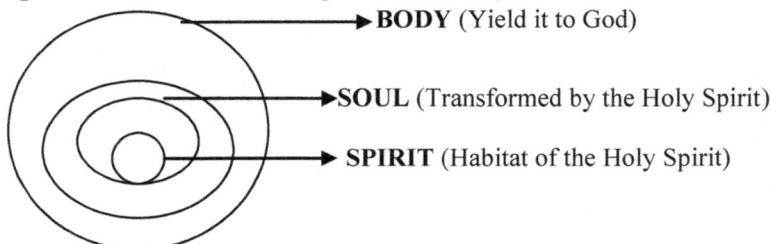

BODY (Yield it to God)

SOUL (Transformed by the Holy Spirit)

SPIRIT (Habitat of the Holy Spirit)

When your mind (soul) is transformed and it submits to the human spirit, which the Holy Spirit in turn controls, it results in the *transformed character* and the person becomes a *spiritual man*. The Holy Spirit does not change our natural disposition or temperament. He builds our strengths and works on our weaknesses (puts them to death) so that they no longer remain obstacles to a godly character. Hence, we become more and more like Christ – Christlikeness.

The Bible uses several words to define temperaments.
- The natural man: 1 Corinthians. 2: 14.
- The carnal nature: Romans 7: 14; 8: 7; 1 Corinthians 3 :1
- The flesh: Romans 8: 3, 9.
- The old man: Romans 6: 6.

■ The outward man: 2 Corinthians 4: 16.

The sin battle

The transformation process mentioned above is not so easy. It is constant work from when one confesses Christ. So long as we live in the flesh, the struggle with our weaknesses manifesting through our character persist. In fact, even the most spiritual persons have yet to attain a level of total yielding, surrender or deliverance. The apostle Paul describes the spiritual struggle as follows:

> *'We know that the law is spiritual; but I am unspiritual, sold as a slave to sin. I do not understand what I do. For what I want to do I do not do, but what I hate I do'*
> *(Romans 7 :14-15)*

When we disobey, gossip, murmur, or get angry, is it Christ in us? No! It is the natural man. We often hear expressions like this; *'It is my natural weakness, I have tried but I cannot do without. I was born like that'!* Yes; Temperament is what is inherited – **the Genotype** - and is manifested through our character and personality. We need to be conscious of our weaknesses to work on them as we daily yield in prayer and submission to the transforming power of the Holy Spirit.

Classification of temperaments

The simplest and easiest recognized classification is that of *Extroverts* and *Introverts*. Many scientists, sociologists, psychologists and philosophers through the years have developed different classifications, using different words. Most scholars today agree on four basic temperamental groups as illustrated by the chart below.

Table 2.1: Classification of temperamental types

System and Author:	D	I	S	C
Career Pathways, Ellis	DOMINANT	INFLUENCING	STEADY	CONSCIENTIOUS
DISC Personal Profile System TM (Carlson Learning Company), Geier:	DOMINANCE	INFLUENCING	STEADINESS	CAUTIOUNESS

Personal DIS-Cernement Inventory (Team Resources inc,) Mohler	DOMINANCE	INFLUENCE	STEADINESS	COMPLIANCE
CARD Personality Style, Rickerson:	DOMINANT D	RELATIONAL R	AMIABLE A	CONSCIENTIOUS C (CARD)
Personal Styles Merrill / Reid:	DRIVER	EXPTRESSIVE	AMIABLE	ANALYTIVAL
Geek Philosopher, Hippocrates, La Haye / Littaur	CHOLERIC	SANGUINE	PHLEGMATIC	MELANCHOLIC
Animal, Smalley / Trent:	LION	OTTER	GOLDEN RETRIEVER	BEAVER

In our study, we are going to use the **DISC classification,** which is widely acclaimed by most authors because it is very descriptive of the temperamental types. However, from time to time, we will refer to the other classification types when need arises. In the following two chapters, we will expose the four basic temperament types under the two generally accepted headings, extroverts and introverts.

EXTROVERTS:
- *Influential (sanguine, expressive, relational)*
- *Dominant (Choleric, Lion, Driver)*

INTROVERTS:
- *Conscientious (Melancholic, Analytical perfectionist)*
- *Steady (Phlegmatic, Amiable, Retriever)*

No one is 100% of one temperament. Usually, one temperament overshadows the others. For example, one may be 50% Influential, 30% Dominant, 15% Conscientious and 5% Stable. Each temperament has strengths (to be encouraged) and weaknesses (to ameliorate). It should be evident that the purpose of this study is not for one to analyze the temperaments of others, but for one to see one's self in the light of God's word and allow the Holy Spirit transform one's weaknesses. Let us now turn to the world of our personality types.

CHAPTER 3
Know Your Personality Type – Part I:
Extroverts

Extroverts are very expressive, be it verbally, emotionally or in action. Their energetic presence is easily felt because they would not remain effaced. They spice the environment by their energy, zeal, enthusiasm, activities, entertainment and distractions. Yet, their dynamism needs proper guidance for maximum and positive production. Let us look at these two outgoing personalities.

Mr. or Miss Influential - Happiness communicator
Mr. Influential is a happy and zealous personality who likes to impress people by his expressions and desires to influence people positively. He is the heart of the party, making people feel welcomed, happy and relaxed in his presence. He is also persuasive and motivating. His major weakness is that he is more of a talkative than a realizer. Below are some of his personality strengths:

1. **Enjoys life**: He loves to enjoy life in the present and would not want anything to disturb this preoccupation. He would quickly do whatever is possible to take away any obstacles or opposition that stands in the way of his cheerfulness.

2. **Very optimistic**: He always sees the positive side of things and usually hopes that things would work. I worked with such a person on a project and his language about the job and the future success was always so exaggeratedly positive.

3. **He is very friendly**: He is good at making friends wherever he is, but also easily forgets them as soon as he leaves. He enjoys the company of others, and inspires confidence wherever he is.

4. **He is compassionate**: He is ready to help by sacrificing himself for others and their problems. He easily understands and sympathizes with others because he is emotional. He easily goes out of his way to help.

5. **He is generous** with what he has. He is emotionally moved to give. He is also generous with his words and can impress

people. He always wants to be at the center of any conversation. He is appreciative, and easily asks for forgiveness and seeks reconciliation.

6. **He is a peacemaker:** Everywhere he is; he wants to make peace among disagreeing parties. He is even ready to take the blame if that would procure peace. Because of this quality, he easily forgives as well as asks for forgiveness.

7. **He is emotional**: He reacts emotionally to circumstances and so can easily be deceived to empty his purse to meet others' needs. He also takes decisions spontaneously.

Mr. Influential is happy, enthusiastic and optimistic and loves life. He is talkative. He is open and so emotionally receptive that what happens to others touches him and leads him to react promptly and without much reflection. **Influentials** make good husbands and homemakers, because of their openness, optimism, and concern for others. Their loveable company, their desire to please their spouse and their ability to forgive or easily ask for forgiveness, makes them pleasant personalities. They are, however, very tender and over flexible. Let us see some of their weak points.

Mr. or Miss Influential's weaknesses - Lack of self-control, impatience

1. **Indiscipline**: Mr. Influential is a good talkative and often talks uncontrollably. Everywhere he is, he monopolizes the conversation. He talks loudly and often is more of a nuisance than a real entertainer. They have to learn to listen more than they talk. They should learn to monitor the environment and shut down when no one is listening. They need to be sensitive to the environment because they often intrude in conversations that do not concern them. Indiscipline manifests in their lack of self-control. Most of them cannot control their appetite and thereby eat excessively and grow out of size. They can also easily build skyscrapers in the air, making promises that they cannot fulfill.

2. **Agitated**: They are always on the move. They are active, but actively doing nothing productive. The English saying,

"Jack of all trades but master of none" properly fits them. They are fun of either beginning programs or projects, but usually abandoning them half way because of difficulties encountered or because of different attractions.

3. **Disorganised**: An influential housewife's kitchen and home as well as the influential's office and desk are disorderly. Things are scattered everywhere, and what is interesting is that they take pleasure in disorder. When you enter the room of a sanguine student, it is apparently obvious because the place may be messy or disorganized. They are prompt at making promises, but usually find it hard to keep them. They also take decisions impulsively without forethought and because of this eventually they realize they cannot sustain the decision. Spiritually, they are agitated and are neither deep nor productive.

4. **Weak Minded**: They are weak-willed and cannot take firm decisions and stand by them. Instead, they can easily be convinced and deviated from their course of action. Because they find it difficult to take firm resolutions, they easily give up when confronted by obstacles and prefer the easier way out. As Christians, they are easily swayed by false doctrines or sensational spiritual activities.

5. **Compromises:** Because they do not want to hurt, they easily compromise in order to please everybody.

6. **Forgetful**: They easily forget their resolutions, appointments and obligations. They are not the best persons to be trusted to follow up a program to success. They also waste lots of time trying to sort out things, or to find out where they have gone astray.

7. **Emotional Instability**: They have many problems controlling their sexual instincts and since they are weak-will, they are easily trapped in lust, fornication, adultery and prostitution. They can be very moody, oscillating from one extreme to the other. For instance, at one moment they would easily shed tears, but soon after would be jumping for joy. They expect others to sympathize with them as they do with others and would feel hurt when it does not happen.

Biblical example of the influential - The Apostle Peter

He was the spokesperson of the disciples and always the first to speak in every situation. Some of the things he said were wonderful, but others just sounded stupid and unreasonable. An example of the latter took place on the mount of transfiguration when he talked of building three tents for Jesus and his heavenly guests without reasoning what it entailed. Was that Jesus' purpose of coming? Would heavenly beings suddenly become earthly creatures and mingle with men? His utterance was just an unreasonable blurt. He often acted spontaneously and that made him unique in many ways. He was the only one apart from his Master who walked upon the sea; he was one of the closest disciples to Jesus and was the medium of some of God's spiritual declarations. Nevertheless, he also quickly pulled out his sword to cut the ear of Marchus when Jesus was arrested. As emotional as he was, he cried out his lungs after denying the Savior three times. On the day of Pentecost, after the Holy Spirit baptism, while others were still wondering what to do when the crowd gathered to mock at them, he appointed himself preacher of the day, quickly stood up before the crowd and gave a sound extemporaneous evangelistic message that brought more than three thousand persons to the Lord in one go.

*****

Sanguines or Influentials can be very good husbands or wives because of their outgoing ability, spontaneity, flexibility, forgiving spirit and ability to understand the other person. They, however, need to work on their weaknesses in order to improve their output. When under the Holy Spirit's anointing and influence, they can be mighty tools in the hands of the Lord. They make good orators, and with anointing, they can be good evangelists, preachers, and Bible teachers. In the circular world, they sell high as journalists, animators, advertisers, public figures, politicians, medical staff and public relations officers. In fact, they are good at social jobs that have to do with being in constant contact with other people. Sanguines are a real spice to society. Thank God if you are one of them and pray that God will make you more organized and productive.

Meet Mr. or Miss Dominant - Hard working hard-liners

Mr. Dominant is an important imposing personality to meet. His presence anywhere is very remarkable because he is not only outspoken, but also very practical, bold and adventurous. If ever people were born leaders, then he is one. He is a man of success and is determined to triumph no matter what it would cost him. Be watchful with him because he can use you to achieve his aims and then dump you. He can also be very strong willed and his fits of anger may be very dangerous. I will like you to meet Mr. Dominant in all his personality.

Mr. Dominant's Personality Strengths

1. **Firm will:** Unlike Mr. or Miss Influential, who can easily be tossed about, Mr. Dominant, is a man of his will. He is firm, resolute and steady. Once he has taken a decision, you would need a bulldozer to move him from it. He is confident of himself and does not give up once he is determined.
2. **Workaholic and practical:** Mr. Dominant is fast, active, practical, and available. He readily volunteers when others sign up. He is a person of action. Enjoying life for him is working and succeeding. He thinks, plans, encourages, works and is always in the lead. He is hard working, organizes things, but does not bother for details.
3. **Born leaders:** Everywhere Dominants find themselves; they seek to be in the lead. They are not just enthusiastic but really make good leaders because they are goal-oriented and motivators. Unlike the Influential personality who would flatter you to give the best of yourself while he oversees, Dominants usually roll up their sleeves and take the lead. As leaders, they succeed more than other personality groups because of their ambition and steadiness, but it is important to note here that in their effort to get ahead, they wound many and abandon others after exploiting them.
4. **Very optimistic:** They are good people to work with because of their optimism. They do not see failure or obstacles; neither do they look at details when it comes to planning. This lack of precaution often lands them into real

difficulties, but they would always find a way out of any situation. This high sense of optimism leads us to the next quality.

5. **Pioneers:** Dominants are bulldozers. They are the ones needed to begin any work that looks daunting. Most of the early missionaries, and explorers such as David Livingston, Hudson Taylor, William Carey and Zingraff were Dominant personalities. I am particularly challenged by the story of William Carey, a British, considered as the father of modern missions. As first missionary to India, he encountered all kinds of difficulties and misfortunes - a debilitating twelve year depression of his first wife that ended in her death, the death of three of his dear children, and that of the second wife, repeated diseases and extreme poverty. He, however, never gave up, but persevered and despite his low level of education (village school education), he accomplished a great deal. In thirty-eight years of missionary toil and sleepless nights, he studied several languages, developed their alphabets, and translated the Bible into forty-two languages and dialects. He opened three missionary stations, established several schools and became an authority in horticulture and agriculture in India. He was a purpose-driven bulldozer, ready to get rid of any obstacle that came between him and his vision. In fact, *'Smaller Trent'* in his classification (see DISC temperament classification in chapter 2) describes Dominants as lions, because they are bold and fearless, being rather encouraged by opposition. Adversity spurs them on as it would a wounded lion. They are daring and adventurous.

6. **Self-sufficient:** While Influentials depend on others, Dominants are self-reliant and can make their way through life. They are self-made men and women. They find it difficult to accept Christ because they do not quite need Him. Even after believing they are so strong-willed that they can do all things without Christ (The opposite of Philippians 4:13). However, there is no limit to their spiritual drive when they learn to lean on God and walk in the Spirit.

Mr. Dominant's Weaknesses: Impatience, Lacks Gentleness

1. *Lack of compassion:* Dominants lack interests in others and do not consider resolving problems with others in love. In fact, they would not bother to make peace. They are uncompassionate.

2. *Wrathful and vengeful:* They can become violently angry and allow their anger to explode. They find it difficult to control their wrath and consequently are very dangerous when angry. A male dominant would easily use his fists, but a female would use her mouth. A Dominant would not shy away from problems. He is not at peace unless he finds a solution, and because of this attitude, he may easily develop stomach ulcers. Naturally, Dominants would do everything to revenge or vent on others. But as believers, their bitterness, anger and vengefulness sadden the Holy Spirit.

3. *Cruel*: A Dominant's cruelty can cause him to despise others, or to be too hard on them. He uses people and then dumps them. He can be very sadistic - causing others to suffer. It must however be underlined that his cruelty is usually unintentional but just an unconscious flow of his personality.

5. *Imprudent and unappreciative*: He easily gets himself entangled in serious problems because he is not prudent. He positively thinks of his ability and prowess without foreseeing any obstacles. Because of his pride, he hardly appreciates things done by others. Instead, he expects others to praise him. He is not at all generous with compliments, especially to his close associates. As a husband, when angry and cannot use his fists on his wife, he adopts verbal abuse which is as harmful.

6. *Self-sufficient*: He is independent and bossy. His self-confidence usually leads to pride and a domineering attitude. His self-conceitedness is a deterrent to his dependence on God. Bible meditation and prayer to him seems a waste of time.

7. *Egoistic:* He is selfish and self-centered. He wants others to give to him but never gives anything away except to promote his personal interest.

Biblical example: Saint Paul

He was already very industrious as an unbeliever. Rare as it was in those days, he was a university graduate with great ambition. As a Pharisee, he thought the Priests and Scribes were not doing their work to exterminate this new sect called the Way. He therefore resolved to become a leading persecutor of the Church. After his encounter with Christ on the Damascus road, he immediately began his spiritual ministry with a three-day fast. After recovering his sight when Ananias prayed for him, he started preaching in that very town, which he had received authorization to persecute. He did not foresee the consequences. As a pioneer, he carried out three missionary journeys and started many churches. He was not deterred by persecution, problems, or pain. Under the anointing of the Holy Spirit, he did excellently and, as he reports, he worked harder than all the other apostles did. He wrote more than half of the books in the *New Testament*. He refused marriage because he saw it as an obstacle to his call. He rejected John Mark for the second missionary journey and even quarreled and separated with Barnabas his disciple maker and mentor. He also ignored the prophetic warning of Agabus not to go to Jerusalem and that earned him serious persecution when he arrived there. Besides these few cases of Dominant weaknesses, Saint Paul was a real leader, greatly used by God. He wrote fourteen of the twenty-seven books of the *New Testament*, pioneered evangelization and church planting in Asia. He also carried out three powerful missionary journeys despite the great odds of his day, trained many young ministers and sent them out to minister, and preached the gospel to many authorities.

*****

Dominants make good, hard-working husbands or wives; they can be good breadwinners or virtuous women such as described in Proverbs 31. They usually succeed in life materially. They are very strong-willed, have no sense of humor, and no time for leisure. Even their children suffer because they have no time to nurture them, since they are constantly under pressure to work. This is often a serious handicap in the family. In society, Dominants excel as pioneer workers, explorers, engineers, large-scale farmers, industrial workers and in other jobs that need hard work and building from scratch. They make good leaders, but not good managers. As leaders, they are able to plan, forecast and take the lead in effecting change in society, but they usually need others as managers to take care of the details and supervise the people working with them. If that is not done, the Dominants would brutalize them. However, under the influence and transforming power of the Holy Spirit, there can be no limit to their exploits.

CHAPTER 4
Know Your Personality Type – Part II: Introverts

Introverts are very peaceful and easygoing personalities. They are calm and reserved and hardly have the urge to confide in others. They make up the profound side of society because their sense of judgment, analysis, interpretation and understanding of events makes them able to plan and foresee possible dangers that lie ahead of any project. However, they are so meticulous and cautious that it is often difficult to trigger them into action because they see more thorns than roses. However, when one succeeds to convince them to act, they often make some of the best professionals and leaders. Under this group falls the Conscientious or Melancholics, on the one hand, and the Steady or Phlegmatics, on the other. Let us look at the two personalities separately.

Meet Mr. or Miss Conscientious - A cautious faithful perfectionist

Miss Conscientious is a careful, observant, cautious, analytic personality with high standards of perfection. She applies these standards both for herself and for those that are with her or under her authority. She is not boisterous, but prefers a quiet reserved life-style. She would prefer not to do anything until someone discovers that she is a talented genius who if convinced would produce a masterpiece.

Personality strengths of Miss Conscientious
1. *Cautious and analytical:* The Conscientious individuals do not quickly commit themselves because they analyze every project, situation, or plan carefully. Their study of a situation often leads them to focus more on the obstacles than on the solutions. They do not take things at their face value, but are always reading between the lines and analyzing the facts and very often wrongly. They are fussy.
2. *Perfectionist:* They always want to give the best of themselves in whatever they desire to accomplish.

Unfortunately, since they are not confident of themselves, they see too many obstacles. Consequently, it is very difficult to convince them to start anything, since the fear of failure or poor results plagues them constantly. However, when they finally accept to do something, you can be sure of the best quality because they would put their all in the task. They shy away from leadership, but when finally convinced to lead, they make some of the best world leaders because of their thoughtfulness, caution and perfectionist tendencies. In most cases, however, they prefer to be faithful followers.

3. *Faithful:* The Conscientious can be fully trusted. They make faithful friends, and unlike the Influentials, who forget their friends as soon as they are out of sight, the Conscientious make lasting friends. This is because, as friends, they have a high sense of duty and self-sacrifice. They make very faithful marriage partners and good associates. At work, they can be quite creative, often proving to be geniuses.

4. *Orderly*: They are very cautious, clean, and orderly, making sure that everything is at its rightful place. When a Conscientious personality uses any article, she makes sure she puts it back in its place. Their houses are usually clean and well kept. Being very meticulous, they respect time scrupulously in contrast to Mr. Influential who is almost always late because of indiscipline. Doing the right thing at the right time is of utmost importance to them. They are very responsible, and expect the same from others.

5. **Cool Emotions:** This personality is as emotional as the Influential. Though less expressive, he is better than the Dominant who hardly exhibits any tender feelings. His emotions however, are at the cool end and more internal than expressive. They are very pensive and moody. They would hardly explode in ecstasy or in tears as the Influential, but would gently, meditatively and quietly slip into frustration, a depressive mood or one of abnegation. Sensitive as they are, they may not react in a given situation, but would be seething inside with anger or dying silently of

remorse. You have to win their absolute confidence before they can open up to you.

Miss Conscientious' Weaknesses - A successful failure

Others envy the Conscientious personality except themselves. While others see them as very successful, they instead view themselves as failures and this perception of themselves can slowly drown them in depression.

1. *Self-centered*: They do a lot of introspection and self-condemnation, paralyzing themselves from action. This introspection bothers them, but they cannot help it. It is unavoidable.

2. *Very Suspicious*: They will easily suspect that others are gossiping about them and draw wrong conclusions. Since they are analytical and pensive, they would read wrongly between the lines. They are good at storing facts and remembering the evil of others even after several years. That is what Esau did with his brother Jacob. Even after twenty years of separation, he had neither forgotten nor forgiven the wrong of his brother.

3. *Complexes*: They can develop either a superiority complex because of the perfectionist tendency, or an inferiority complex because of the fear of failure. This is dangerous because it either moves them to despise others or to develop self-pity that leads to depression and even suicide.

4. *Depressive tendencies:* This is obvious from the above analysis. They capitalize on their failures, would not see the 90% success but the 10% failure and that can ruin them. A Melancholic would complain repeatedly of that which is going wrong and would make no effort to correct it. He would sink into periods of despair and even depression without apparent cause (just because of much reflection and analysis). This attitude embarrasses their marriage partner or colleagues because it is frustrating.

5. *Pessimistic:* Their analytical tendency is often more pessimistic than optimistic because they focus on the bad side of the story. They would therefore make a big deal out of the smallest mistake and magnify problems out of

proportion. This causes them to be undecided and frightened to embark on new projects, and to dampen others' enthusiasm. They would quickly throw ice water on any new project.

6. *Imprudent and unappreciative*: Because of his perfectionist tendency, he sets unattainable standards for his wife, children and associates. This traumatizes the children and dampens the wife's enthusiasm because of their inability to satisfy him. He himself in turn would become depressed and everyone suffers. The smallest errors of wife, husband or children are magnified and capitalized on.

7. *Vengeful*: They have an unforgiving spirit. They would keep, accumulate, remember, and analyze, the wrongs of others and can pour out the catalogue, or replay the tape when necessary. Even when they forgive, they do not forget. They may appear outwardly calm and quiet, but will be seething inside with anger, hatred and revenge – and can remain this way for years. They may rarely explode in anger as the Dominant personality studied in the previous chapter but would conceal their judgment or negative perception of others indefinitely.

Biblical Examples: **Moses, *Elijah, King Solomon, and Apostle John***

The Conscientious personality has a very rich temperament, and with the anointing of the Holy Spirit, they can go far. Moses is a typical example. He did not want to commit himself to the task to which God was calling him. He analyzed the situation and resisted God's call to such a point that God became angry. We see that in *Exodus* 3 from verse 11:

Verse II '*Who am I that I should go to Pharaoh and that I should bring the children of Israel out of Egypt?*'
Verse 13 '*When they say to me what is his name? What shall I say to them?*'
Chapter 4: 1 '*But suppose they will not believe me or listen to my voice, or say the Lord has not appeared to you.*'
Chapter 4: 13 '*Oh my Lord please send another*'

He was not ready to commit himself. However, when he finally did, he performed excellently. I do not know whether we have any leader in the *Old Testament* who is better than he is. He bore the people, fasted and prayed for them. When God, in his anger, wanted to destroy the Israelites in the wilderness, he stood in the gap for them. He had a perfect ministry. He was faithful to the end.

*****

The Conscientious make faithful husbands or wives. They are very committed and caring, but set high standards for their spouses and children. They are very orderly; they would prefer not to eat because the meal is not the right one or because it is not to their taste. As rich as this temperament is, so also are its weaknesses. One has to guard against these weaknesses by submitting to the transforming power of the Holy Spirit; otherwise, depression and even suicide are great potential dangers.

Melancholics perform well in jobs that require thinking, analysis, planning and invention. They make excellent scientists, artists of all kinds, administrators, managers, bankers, designers, accountants and clerical officers. They do not relate to people as easily as Extroverts, but are at their best with figures, books, computers, and other inanimate equipment that permit them to exhibit their ingenuity. They are absolutely trustworthy and reliable.

Mr. or Miss Steady - Conservative, Calm and Steadfast

No temperament is more balanced than Mr Steady is. He is not an extremist. He is not agitated, fussy, or inquisitive. He is cool, nice and easygoing. He would not want you to intrude in his affairs, nor would he intrude in those of others. That is, he minds his business and expects others to do same. He is a loveable person because he is not a troublemaker but slow, steadfast and steady. He is annoyed by the talkative nature of the Influential, the forwardness of the Dominant, and the negative comments of the Conscientious, but he sits on the fence not bothering to voice out his opinion. Let us look at his personality strengths and weaknesses:

Mr. Steady's Personality Strengths
1. *Effective:* His effectiveness is the type that enables him to do just that which is required. He is not a man of excesses and so would not waste energy on trifles as would the extrovert. He is a born practical economist with an aversion to extravagance. He would use minimum effort to attain his objectives.
2. *Steady and stable:* People with this temperament are very balanced in life in almost every aspect. As Christians, they are not easily carried away by any new wind of doctrine. They would not easily accept new things whether good or bad. In a way, it is a good quality, but when it is carried to the extreme the Steady become purely conservative, refusing any changes, be they positive or negative. So long as the old method still works, they see no need for change. They are not as easily disturbed as people with the other temperaments. A Steady or Phlegmatic personality is always himself regardless of the changes occurring around him. Steady personalities do not express their emotions; that is, with them, there is no explosive laughter or outburst of anger.
3. *Friendly and humorist:* They love the company of others and have a good sense of cool humor. In a conversation, they can easily crack jokes that would make others laugh out their lungs while they would remain calm and unshaken. They are experts at imitating others and usually make good actors because they would act naturally. They are humorists and usually use that to mock at others or to provoke them.
4. **Calm, slow, and cool:** Worrying is not part of their vocabulary. They are unshakeable and very sure of themselves. During one of my medical consultations, a mother came into my office with a Phlegmatic son of about two years and placed him on an armless chair while lying on an examination bed for an ultrasound scan. My secretary alerted her that the baby might fall. But she assured her it

would not happen. Amazed, we all observed this baby for the next twenty minutes as he sat at the same spot just twisting his hands from time to time, but making no effort to reach out for his mother or to cry out for help.

5. **A good observer:** They stand aloof and see others act and react. They do not commit themselves, but come in to mock when things fail. *"I knew it would fail "*, they would say.

6. **Qualified Leaders:** When pushed into leadership they prove very capable, balanced and qualified. As leaders, they are peacemakers and reconcilers. They make excellent managing leaders, balance teachers, cautious diplomats and effective accountants.

Mr. Steady's weaknesses – Sluggish, lazy, and conservative

1) **Slow**: People with this personality are slow to take decisions, slow to act, slow to commitments and usually late. They lack motivation and zeal. They would virtually take twice as much time as others to do a particular job. Schoolteachers have to make an extra effort to be patient with children of this temperamental group.

2) *Lazy*: As long as it is possible not to work, they would love to sit around doing nothing. Given that they are often undecided, they would prefer to sit on the fence and make no effort except forced to do so.

3) *A thorn in the flesh*: They are very sarcastic and provocative. They delight in watering down the efforts of others.

4) **Stubborn and strong-willed**: Unlike the Dominant personality that is overtly strong-willed, this group is silently stubborn, opposing all effort to change. Also tight fisted, they would not want to spend on others, or invite you for a meal. They would not spend except when necessary. They are very self-centered in all their decisions. *"I"* is in the center of their all. They are born economist.

5) **Indecision**: These personality types are very undecided on several issues because they do not want to pay the price. Indecision becomes a habit and makes them slothful and unproductive.

6) **Conservative:** They are enemies of change. So long as the old method or technique works, they do not see why one should desire a change. This is because they are afraid it would need their effort and probably finances.

Biblical examples

- ◆ **Andrew** has only twelve biblical quotations against his younger brother Peter's one hundred. We see from the same family two different temperaments.
- ◆ **James:** Nothing much is said about him because he was not an outspoken man. While his brother Jesus was around, we do not hear of him believing in Him, but later on we see that he believed and became the leader of the council of the church in Jerusalem. He is also the author of the profound *Book of James*. (Act 12: 17 Act 15: 13, Gal 2: 9.)

*****

This personality type is most effective under stress or pressure. As husbands or wives, they live a very balanced life and would not stir up any quarrel or allow themselves to be provoked by their spouse. They, however, need a push when it comes to planning the future of the family, or solving emergencies. In this wise, it is advisable for a steady personality to get married to an extrovert in order to strike a balance, otherwise life would be monotonous and unproductive.

In the circular world, they function best as managers of corporations and organizations, balancing all aspects of the business and preventing it from collapsing. One would not expect any giant breakthroughs under their leadership, as they are neither visionaries, nor motivators, nor vectors of change. They serve best in routine jobs that need neither much reflection nor innovations. They can also be good followers because they would remain steadfast. If everybody in the world were a phlegmatic, there would be no outbreaks of war and no turmoil. The world would be a peaceful place to live in but it would also be boring and monotonous.

CHAPTER 5
Overcoming Your Personality Weaknesses

Before we discuss how we can overcome our weaknesses, let us look at some real examples of families with temperament clashes.

Mr. Dominant and Mrs. Conscientious

Mr. William Carey as mentioned in an earlier as the founder of modern missions, surmounted many obstacles. He and his first wife Dorothy spent most of their fruitful years in India as pioneer missionaries. While he succeeded brilliantly as a missionary because of his dominant nature, he failed as a husband and father. Despite his insignificant educational status and poor financial resources, he determined to get his family across the oceans from Britain to India as missionaries. Every external factor was against his adventurous proposal. The missionary board rejected the idea for several years, but he persisted. The church he was pasturing did not see with him, but he stood firm. His parents were vehemently opposed and even considered him mad, yet he did not bother. Finally, his wife was adamant in her decision. *"I am not going"*, she violently resisted. But he was undeterred by all the refusal and opposition. This can be seen in a letter to his father quoted by William J. Petersen in his book "Martin Luther had a wife",

'I have many sacrifices to make. I must part with a beloved family and a number of most affectionate friends. Never did I see such sorrow manifested as reigned through our place of worship last Lord's Day. But I have set my hand to the plough.' Though he finally travelled with his wife, he had initially determined to leave her back in England for three years with some of his children and take along their eight-year-old son.

Dorothy on her part was a refined analytical and conscientious woman. Already while in Britain, she had suffered depressive crises because of her impulsive, imprudent and negligent husband. Shortly after marriage, they had lost their first and only daughter. It profoundly injured her psychologically. While her husband was hopping excitedly from one town to another to preach, she was dying at home alone for want of love, security and attention. You can then understand that after a careful analysis of their few years of marriage, she could not give in to this crazy, reckless and imprudent decision to take the family to India. She saw her husband as an unsuccessful adventurer. In their first twelve years of marriage, they had moved on four different occasions, and still had no permanent residence. He had changed jobs eight times. He was unstable and agitated. When he wanted his wife to travel with him to India, she was five months pregnant and could not imagine boarding a ship in that condition. In addition to the normal risks at sea, there was then a conflict between France and Britain, and any British ship at sea ran the risk of attack by France. Though it was very unusual in those days for a wife to oppose her husband's decision, she could not after such detail analysis consent to go along with an imprudent husband on this suicidal trip – which finally turned out to be.

Finally, under extreme pressure and after delivering, she unwillingly accepted to go along with the children. With this decision, she signed her death warrant. While her body went along, her mind snapped. She lived for fourteen years in India before dying, but only the first two years were less stressful. With the extreme poverty and misery they had to cope with, the frequent moving (they moved six times within the first nine months), the degrading health conditions which they all experienced especially the children, and finally the death of two of their children. Her condition painfully and gradually deteriorated from stress to depression, and to neurosis and finally to mania. She spent the last twelve years of her life in this miserable state, while her husband kept going as if everything was all right. She finally passed away after many years of house confinement.

If her husband had been a melancholic, he would have carried the guilt of her death all his life, but as a Choleric, he shook it off and remarried barely six months later. His untiring purpose-driven efforts hidden in his life slogan, **'expect great things from God, attempt great things for God'** yielded dividend. In thirty-eight years of missionary labor, he developed the alphabet of several languages and translated the Bible into forty-two languages and dialects. He also started several mission stations, established schools, and became an outstanding reference in horticulture and agriculture in India. William Carey might have been a failure in business, teaching, and fatherhood, he might have failed as a husband, but he achieved his heart's desire as a missionary. The weaknesses that characterize a Melancholic overshadowed any strength in the life of his wife and she suffered and died under the strenuous, hard-driven lifestyle engineered by her husband. One left an impressive impact while the other left behind painful memories.

Mr. Influential and Mrs. Steady

Mr. Jack has been married for over ten years and has more than five children. He and his wife have jobs and earn reasonable salaries. Yet Jack is always in financial problems. He finds it difficult to pay his bills, and meet the family needs. This is so because he has not outgrown his compulsive generosity. He is emotionally moved to meet the needs of those that approach him and since he has been known for this weakness, the number of people that approach him for help always overwhelms him. He has made no investment for all his years of work– no savings, no landed property, no house, nothing.

Jack is, however, a very pleasant person, always looking happy and excited about little things. He loves to sing and is a very good musician, but does not have enough time to develop this talent. He loves to be at the heart of every conversation. He also is so available that he gets himself entangled with too many meetings, rendezvous, and out-of-home activities. The result is that his children miss him and are constantly complaining.

Matilda, his wife, is more regular at home, because she hardly involves herself in out-of-home activities. She prefers the quiet side of life and keeps such a low profile that even when she is somewhere you would not feel her presence. She would not talk, act or react. Their children complain that she is too quiet and inexpressive except when it comes to scolding them. They are neglected and do as they please. Most often, they are shabby and unkempt as they struggle to meet their needs outdoors. Matilda's living room is untidy and disorderly. She does not bother to be hospitable to their visitors since, in addition to her sluggishness, and apart from their financial plight, she is stiff handed.

Matilda, is sometimes forced into position of leadership and, when that happens, she begins well but soon proves to be too hard on her subordinates. She would impose on others and expect them to comply. She is authoritative and finds it difficult to get along with the others. Because of this, she has lost many friends, better job opportunities and some leading positions. Her domineering attitude may be due to the fact that back home her husband allows her to run the show.

How to Overcome Your Weaknesses
1. *Be grateful to God for your temperament* :
It is a God given temperament. No temperament is better than another. The world needs them all. You must not weep over your temperament, but be grateful to the Lord for it. Also, do not think that you are better than others because of your temperament. Philippians 2: 3-4 says, *"Esteem others better than yourself"*. Whatever your temperament, you can make a wonderful spouse and your family can become a success.

2. *Determine to accept and love your fiancée with all his/her weaknesses* :
If you have made up your mind to marry someone, you must be determined to accept and love the person as he/she is while prayerfully hoping he/she works on his/her weaknesses. As the Bible says, true love bears all things. That is a manifestation of the love of God. God loves even his enemies. Ask God for grace to love. Sometimes real natural love flows towards others, yet at other moments we need to ask God for supernatural love for our spouse. (Romans 5: 5, 8: 32*): 'Lord I want to*

love him /her no matter what he/she is or does. I need that supernatural touch of God'.

3. *Recognize and accept your weaknesses :*

Each of us has weaknesses. You have to accept them. There is nothing shameful about that. Once you realize that you have natural weaknesses, you would see the need for a solution. When you understand that your weaknesses are a sore point in your life and future marriage, you would desire a change and that is when God steps in to help you out.

4. *Be practical: Discuss and face your weaknesses*: Follow the points below.

a) Write out your weaknesses. Do not be afraid or intimidated to do this. It would help you to face yourself squarely and see what needs to be done.

b) Write out the strong points and the weaknesses of your future partner; about ten each.

c) Exchange your papers and accept the views of your partner even if you do not agree fully. That is the way he/she sees you and you obviously do not know yourself fully. Moreover, marriage is aimed at pleasing the other person and not yourself. Discuss and pray over them. Ask for God's help.

d) Keep the papers and tick thank God for each of them as you see transformation operated in your life.

5. *Ask for God's intervention:* Below are three important points to consider seriously.

a) Invite Jesus into your life and family. There can be no real successful marriage without Christ. You need Jesus to change your life and :

- Give you victory over your weaknesses.
- Give you grace to bear and love your future partner.
- Give you a forgiving spirit.

b) Consider all your weaknesses as sin. Until you see your weaknesses as obstacles in your life and marriage and determine to radically deal with them, you would not experience fast victory. Therefore, after enumerating them as indicated above, take time to pray and ask God to forgive and deliver you from those weaknesses. Make a careful plan on how to deal with them. The best advice is to starve those weaknesses. That means each time they show up their ugly heads and request that you obey, you determine to do the very opposite. Take for instance if you easily get angry and pronounce curse words, you determine that once the forceful urge to do these things comes up, you prayerfully bury it and do the opposite. This would take time to practice but it would finally yield dividend.

c) You need the help of the Holy Spirit in your life. We cannot do without the help of God. He puts the personality in us and can grant us the ability to overcome the weaknesses. Though Jesus was a perfect man from birth, he still needed to be baptized and receive the Holy Spirit. You also need the fullness of the Holy Spirit in your life. Ask God to fill you with Himself and you will experience Christ and the fruit of the Holy Spirit more and more. "But the fruit of the Spirit is love, peace, longsuffering, gentleness, gentleness, goodness, faith, meekness, temperance: against such there is no law. And they that are Christ's have crucified the flesh with the affections and lusts. Galatians 5:22-24)

Change will not be spontaneous or radical. No! God fills you when you ask Him, but the change in character weaknesses will be a daily process as the Spirit of God leads you through different circumstances of life (James 1: 12). Let us see how it happened in the lives of some Bible characters.

Biblical Examples
Moses: Had a carnal choleric attitude from the onset. It even led him to kill an Egyptian who had a scuffle with an Israelite. Then he had an encounter with God. And was transformed with time to become the meekest man on earth such that when God wanted to destroy the Israelites in the wilderness because of their disobedience, he stood in the gap and pleaded for them. He was ready to die for those he was called to lead. He was so meek that when Aaron and Miriam accused him of getting

married to an Ethiopian, he did not fight back. God had to defend him. That was not the attitude of the carnal Moses we knew before. The Holy Spirit had done a deep work in his life. Though anger never completely disappeared, the outbursts that caused him to kill from the onset were no longer a threat.

Peter: He was talkative, carnal, spontaneous and impulsive. He even denied his Master Jesus before a simple housemaid. After the death of Jesus, he was tempted to go back to the world, to his old profession. The turning point in his life came after his repentance after denying Jesus and later on at the baptism of the Holy Spirit. He was then transformed into a powerful servant of God by the fruit of the Holy Spirit. He was endowed with boldness and perseverance. He became an effective preacher, pastor, leader and writer. That is what the Holy Spirit can do to anyone who submits to His sovereignty.

Deliverance From Your Weaknesses – Recapitulation
1. *Consider your weaknesses as sin.*
> Do not give excuses: *'It is my nature or I cannot help it'.* The Bible says *'I can do all things through Christ who strengthens me' (Philippians 4: 13).* Obviously, most of our weaknesses appear as sin before God. It may be depression, fear, anger, lust, jealousy, laziness, impatience, selfishness, indiscipline, disorderliness, lack of submission, unforgiving, pride, exaggeration, hypocrisy, etc. It is a sin for any of such weaknesses to be part of your character.

2. *Confess your sins to God and ask him for deliverance (John 8: 32, 36; Prov. 28: 13).*
> Learn to confess your sin each time it manifests itself. Ask God to deliver you from that dirty practice and habit, and continue to pray until you see positive results. Let it weigh on your heart, seek counseling. Co-operate with the Holy Spirit and determine that next time it wants to happen you would immediately turn to God and ask him for self-control.

3. Stand on the word of God and claim your victory (John 5: 14-15).

The Bible says that we shall know the truth and that truth will set us free. Now you know the truth about your nature and the solution that is found in Jesus, the Everlasting Truth. If the Son of God sets you free you will be free indeed. Let Him do that to you. Claim your victory and stand on it.

4. Live constantly under the anointing of God's fullness and the Holy Spirit.

Walk in the Spirit (Galatians 5: 16; John 15: 1-11). Meditation and prayer should characterize your life. If you fall again as regards a particular weakness, do not be discouraged. Consider it as a Christian who has fallen in sin. Re-confess it and remind Satan of the victory of Jesus in your life. Remember, habits are easily formed but difficult to break (1Corinthians 10: 13). Every believer goes through the period of struggling against sin, but one thing we are always sure of is Victory.

> *"For in my inner being I delight in God's law; but I see another law at work in the members of my body, waging war against the law of my mind and making me a prisoner of the law of sin at work within my members. What a wretched man I am! Who will rescue me from this body of death? Thanks be to God -- through Jesus Christ our Lord! So then, I myself in my mind am a slave to God's law, but in the sinful nature a slave to the law of sin" (Romans 7: 22-25).*

CHAPTER 6
Anatomy of Sex Organs and the Pubertal Experience

The pubertal period is a complicated moment in the life of the growing youth because he/she begins to experience changes that are often difficult to handle. This period begins earlier in girls between nine and twelve, but in boys, it takes place between the ages of twelve, and fifteen. The changes that take place are physical, physiological and psychological. What interest us here are the physical and psychological or emotional changes. Since they differ in the both sexes, we will look at them separately.

Pubertal changes in boys

A group of hormones produced by the testes called androgens triggers puberty in boys. The most important of them is called testosterone. These hormones provoke the development of secondary sexual characteristics as follows:

1. The voice begins to deepen and becomes coarser.
2. The chest muscles develop giving the chest a broader appearance.
3. The young man begins to develop body hair concentrated in certain areas, especially the chest, the chin, the armpits and the pubic area.
4. The teenager starts producing sperms by a process called spermatogenesis. From time to time he may have a wet dreams a night in which he wets his pant with semen.
5. The penis develops to a bigger size and the vascularization also increases in order to enable proper erection during coitus.
6. The most difficult change to handle is an emotional one. He starts developing a sexual drive or sentiment towards the opposite sex and this is the crucial moment when the parents have to come in with counsel, otherwise other teenagers would introduce him to an immoral life. This is the period when they must learn to control this God-given emotion. In

our study, young boys are most vulnerable to fall in the sexual sin between the ages of sixteen, and eighteen. 72 per cent of boys in our study lost their virginity before the age of twenty. That is serious and parents must handle their boys with love and firmness.

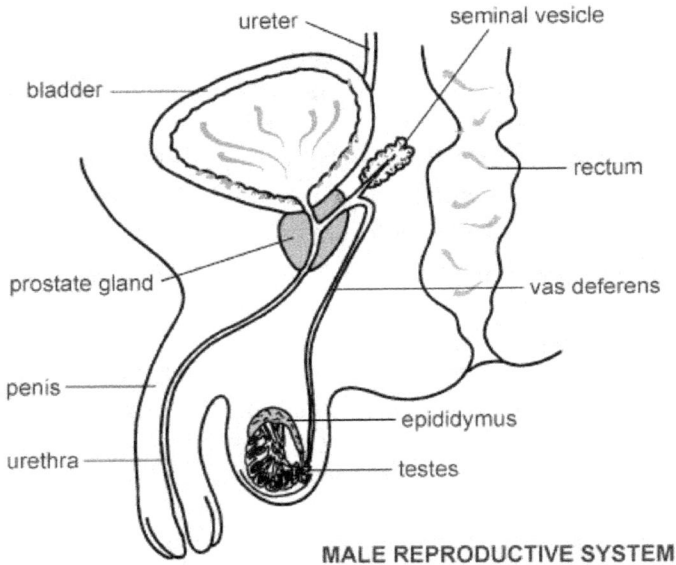

MALE REPRODUCTIVE SYSTEM

Fig 6.1 Anatomy of the male sexual organs

Pubertal Changes in Girls

The girl is more complex when it comes to puberty. To explain it simply, the Pituitary gland in the brain and the ovaries are responsible for the onset of pubertal changes. The ovaries produce a group of hormones called oestrogenes and they are responsible for the physiological changes in the woman. These changes bring about secondary sexual characteristics, which are external, internal, and psychological.

1. *Externally:*
    a) The girl's breast develops and the glandular tissue increases in size as she prepares for womanhood.

b) She develops hair in the armpits and the pubic region.

c) Her skin becomes more tender and smooth as more fat is deposited in the sub cutaneous layer.

2. *Internally:*

   a) The pelvis broadens and the pelvic cavity enlarges in order to prepare for pregnancy and delivery.

   b) The uterus grows rapidly in size, the cavity enlarges, and the walls thicken in preparation for conception. This highly vascularized thickened uterine lining called the endometrium sloughs off ones a month when there is no pregnancy and the woman bleeds in a process called menstruation.

   c) The ovaries become active and through the influence of some hormones begin producing eggs called ova. Every month, one ovary produces an ovum, which moves from the ovary through the fallopian tube into the uterine cavity. The girl's body then prepares for a pregnancy in case she has a sexual contact with a man. If it does not happen, the egg dies off in a few days and the uterine lining sloughs off as menses. Puberty is a dangerous period for girls because they can get pregnant even after a single sexual contact. Contrary to what is taught in primary and some secondary schools, it is quite difficult to predict the safe interval (when a girl cannot get pregnant) because the menstrual cycle differs in every woman.

   d) The vaginal wall or mucosa develops and begins responding to the monthly cycle by producing whitish slimy mucous at particular moments.

3. *Psychologically*

   a) The woman begins to sense womanhood. It varies with persons and environment, but the girls begin to become sensitive to the fact that she is feminine and needs to behave in a certain way. They begin to observe and copy the movement, dressing, and attitudes of their mothers. This is a very important period for the girl because she learns a lot by being close to her mother. Mothers have to be aware of this because if they are not open to advice and teach their daughters at this crucial period, they may copy the wrong persons.

b) The girl starts experiencing a sexual attraction towards the opposite sex. They can be sexually aroused by touch, especially the fondling of their breasts or other sensitive body parts. Here again, parents have to counsel and advise their daughters.

c) They begin to develop a sense of privacy. They would not love to be seen naked or half-exposed and do not appreciate others entering their rooms without knocking.

Fig 6.2: Anatomy of the Female Sexual Organs

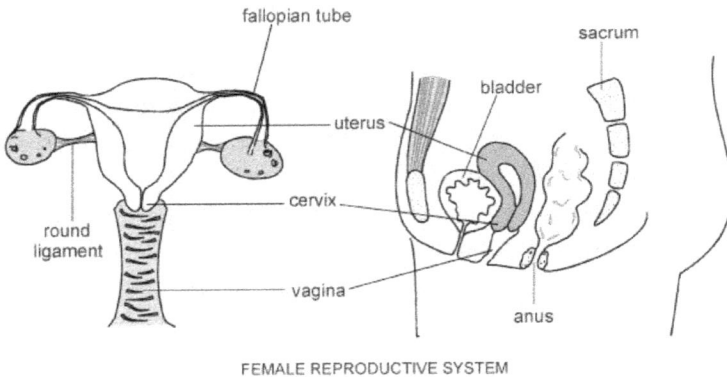

FEMALE REPRODUCTIVE SYSTEM

Body Hygiene

I have realized during my medical consultations that many women and men are very ignorant about taking good care of their bodies and especially of their private parts and external reproductive organs. This results in either offensive odors that some people carry around or unnecessary infections. With foul body odors the youths become ignorantly offensive in church or at gatherings either because of strong body odor or foul mouth stench. It is therefore of prime importance that we, as Christians learn to be neat and take good care of our bodies. Let us look at some aspects one after another.

1. **Care of the mouth.**

    The mouth at every moment has saprophytic germs that are responsible for degradation of any food particles, dead cells or any other degradable substances. A poorly cleaned mouth therefore sends out an unpleasant odor that vitiates the air around. This situation is worse when brethren fast and forget to clean their mouths. Here are a few guidelines:

    a) In the morning when you clean your mouth, you must do the following:

    - Brush not only your teeth but also your gums and especially your tongue. You would often realize that some unbrushed tongues are often coated with a whitish substance. It is a source of bad odor.

    - Remember to brush the back of your mouth, that is, the larynx and cough out all the secretions of dead tissues that collected there overnight (i.e. at the junction between mouth, nose and throat). If these secretions were not coughed out, they would speed up the degradation process in your mouth, producing an odor barely a few hours after you must have brushed your teeth properly.

    - Clear the back of your nasal cavity and empty any secretions that must have accumulated there at night. Also blow your nose.

    b) If you happen to be fasting, then brush your mouth with tooth paste at least once within the day. Otherwise use some local or manufactured mouth refreshers. In our environment, lime, lemon, and bitter cola are good local mouth refreshers.

2. **Care of the face**

    Cleaning of the face is more important for girls than for boys because the skin of the girl's face is prone to storing excess fat. From puberty onward, this sub-cutaneous fat produces pimples. This is more likely for those with tender and light skin than for those with a darker complexion. The nose also stores up some of this fat. If you were to press the two lobes of your nose, you would realize how much fat they accumulate. Those who do not do this regularly tend to have a shiny or furred nose with whitish particles projecting from the pores. Both boys and girls should therefore do this regularly.

Girls should give an additional care to their faces in order to maintain their God given beauty. They should learn to clean their faces every morning and every evening before going to bed. Generally, ordinary bathing soap would do, but for some persons simple skin antiseptic lotions may be necessary. In such cases, advice from more responsible women or medical practitioners should be sought.

3. Care of the armpits and inguinal folds

The armpits and the inguinal folds are very important parts of the body needing proper care. Everybody has a body odor. It is usually stronger for some people, especially for girls, than for others. The armpits and the groins are the main sources of our body odors because those are the areas where we perspire most. If they are not properly cleaned, sweat accumulates on the hair, causing it to turn whitish or brownish, exuding a foul smell. Such individuals have a very strong nauseating body odor, especially after sweating. Therefore, when bathing, these areas should be properly scrubbed with soap and a soft sponge. It is not advisable to shave these parts regularly.

In case you have a strong body odor despite proper body care, it would be necessary to wear a perfume that helps to neutralize it. But it is important to make a good choice because some combinations of perfume and body odor are even more nauseating. People with body odor are also advised to constantly change their clothes, especially after effort or profuse sweating.

Henry is a mechanic and comes home after a hard day's labor, dirty and stinking. His wife, Philo, could not continue to bear his dirty habits because quite often she is surprised that her husband would go to bed without bathing and would even want to have sex with her in such a condition. She came complaining to me. Needless to say that today, even after having had three kids and built a house of their own, they are no longer together. Even such simple unaltered habits can accentuate to break a good marriage

4. For women only

Women need to take additional care of their pubic region. Young girls and adolescents must learn how to clean their vulva region very well. For all virgins, the hymen is still intact and so they should clean the region without sending their fingers into their intimacy. But for women, who have already had a sexual relationship, the hymen is already broken and they should use soap and clean water to douche inside the vaginal cavity. The vagina is not a sterile milieu and so women should not be afraid to use their fingers to clean up. However, their nails must be clean and short.

The use of antiseptic soaps and antiseptic solutions is strongly discouraged. This is because there is a saprophytic bacterium species that gives a particular acidity to the vaginal cavity, thereby preventing infections. But with the abusive use of antiseptics this bacterium species is destroyed and the woman is exposed to all kinds of simple infections.

Finally, when the woman goes to the toilet, she cleans up from the front backwards and not the reverse. If she does the reverse, she would carry germs from the anal area to the vulva and contaminate herself.

5. Care of the skin

Another crucial problem is the care of the skin. Some people especially women use some cosmetic products with the intention of becoming lighter in completion. This is a very destructive habit with regrettable consequences. Before these products cause the desired results, they peel off insidiously the external layer of the epidermis. This skin layer serves to protect the body from external aggression, and to regenerate the skin when there is a wound. Now when this layer is sloughed off, the skin in exposed to all kinds of external aggressions and the victims easily fall prey to skin diseases of fungal, bacterial and viral origin. Moreover, it is not easy for their surface skin to regenerate when there is a wound. I know a few ladies who died after surgical interventions because their skin could not regenerate.

6. Care of the hair

The hair plays a vital role in both women and men, but today with modernization they are so many modifications in hairstyles and dressing. Many young people tend to shave off all their hair rendering the skull as smooth as an egg. These are dangerous habits because the skin of the hair is exposed to eternal aggressions including direct sunrays, fungi infections, and trauma. The shock absorption provided by hair in case of violent trauma is absent and the person is more exposed. The other extreme is the wearing of Rasta thereby keeping the hair unkempt and dirty. Lastly, some people dye their hair, changing the color to brown, orange or gold. The products used are not without side effects and those who use them expose themselves to all the negative side effects, which very often are not immediate but long term. This problem of change of hair color and the use of chemicals is more common with women than men. Most women have naturally beautiful hair and it is an abuse of God's beautiful creation to build additional mountains on your head in the name of fashion. To be honest, most men are put off and not attracted by the make-up on which women spend so much time and money, for, in a good number of cases, the make-up makes them rather ugly. Remember that there is natural beauty that God has created, and it is ALWAYS the best if it is well maintained. Moreover, do not forget the unnecessary expenditure, which is often obligatory even in cases of poverty.

To end this aspect of body hygiene, we should remember that God has made us all in a beautiful variety. No two people are alike. When God made man and woman on the last day of creation, the Bible says he saw that all was very good. God has created you beautiful or handsome depending on your sex. We do not need to add to God's creation because we would be saying, *"God, your work was not perfect, so let me help you to perfect it."* On the contrary, we should maintain, polish, and dress up the beauty of God's creation. And that beauty is **YOU**.

Physical Maturity and Self-Control

In the next chapter, we will explain that for a young person to be ready for marriage he or she has to experience four different kinds of maturity. However, here I want to answer a question that bothers many young people. The question is why God decided to allow physical maturity with this dangerous emotion called sexual instincts to come up long before one is ready for marriage. Why did God not give people these sexual instincts only when they are about to get married? That would have prevented promiscuity, fornication, unwanted pregnancies, and young people would have been free to study without being harassed prematurely by people of the opposite sex.

This is a crucial issue. In the Bible we read the story of a young man called Ammon who was obsessed by his sexual instincts and he wanted at all cost to go to bed with his beautiful half-sister Tamar. The story is found in 2 Samuel 13. Unfortunately, for Ammon, he had a vicious friend who gave him bad counsel. How I wish Jonadab had been a spiritual person. But this vicious friend told him: *"Go to bed and pretend to be ill," Jonadab said. "When your father comes to see you, say to him, 'I would like my sister Tamar to come and give me something to eat. Let her prepare the food in my sight so I may watch her and then eat it from her hand.'"* First of all it was a lie to fake sickness, and secondly it was bad counsel. The Bible says that bad company corrupts good morals. Every youth has to be careful of bad company because it will lead one astray – **into sin.** Adolescents must take this counsel very seriously as they make friends in school, church, and in the society. Bad friend will take you to the wrong places and will push you to do the wrong things – even to commit the sexual sin.

Ammon followed this vicious advice, played the trick and finally forced his sister to bed. After that he sent the sister away and the Bible adds, *"Then Amnon hated her with intense hatred. In fact, he hated her more than he had loved her. Amnon said to her, "Get up and get out" (Verse 15).*

Young ladies, you have to be very careful here. When a young man says, *"I love you."* In fact, in most cases, what he really means is, *"I am lusting after you and want to use you."* In almost all cases when the stupid girls allow themselves to be used by a young man who is in dire need to assuage his sexual drive, they are abused and afterwards abandoned like undesired stuff. Do you understand what I mean? And often, this immoral act leaves the girl with an unwanted product of their sin – *a pregnancy or a psychological trauma.* Girls, you have been warned. Do not give in. The Bible says your body is the temple of the Holy Spirit. Let it remain holy and do not prostitute it.

Now let us come back to our question. Why the presence of sexual instincts so early in life? Sexual instincts are controlled by the mind or soul. But man is made up of the Spirit, soul and body. The spirit is the real you, the soul is the intermediary between the body and the spirit. In fact he is the managing director of your life. The body is the house in which your spirit lives. When emotions are born in the mind, they can either be subject to the spirit – **the real you**, or to the body – **the house.** If they are subject to the spirit, then your spirit would exercise control over them and you would be able to resist them. Especially if your spirit is subject to the Spirit of God living in you, He would grant you self-control so that you would learn to control your instincts. But if you are carnal and are led by the lust of the flesh, then you would not be able to control your sexual drive and would fall in sin. Now, this is what the Bible says, *"Those who live according to the sinful nature have their minds set on what that nature desires; but those who live in accordance with the Spirit have their minds set on what the Spirit desires. The mind of sinful man is death, but the mind controlled by the Spirit is life and peace; the sinful mind is hostile to God. It does not submit to God's law, nor can it do so. Those controlled by the sinful nature cannot please God"* (Romans 5:5-8).

*****

God wants to teach you self-control. A real man is one who can control his appetites, emotions and instincts. If you cannot, I am sorry to say it, you are not better than the dogs outside there. If you commit your life to the Spirit of God He will give you **self-control** and you will be able to control your sexual drive. After all, remember that marriage is not the solution to indiscipline. When one gets married, there are times one cannot enjoy sex because the other partner is indisposed, maybe sick, on a journey, or not in good mood. What would you do if you had not learnt the lesson of self-control? Would you want to do as the other untamed men and women who hide behind big cars, tinted windscreens, or in dark corners to behave like untamed dogs? No! You are worth more than that. You are a precious child of God. God never makes mistakes. He placed the instincts there long before marriage for your good. So that you will learn to be a real man or woman – **one who has developed self-control.**

Take the Joseph's Vow
In Genesis 39, the Bible recounts the story of a handsome young man, Joseph who was enticed daily by his mistress to go to bed with her. Joseph had sexual instincts like every other youth and could have easily fallen prey to this temptation. He could have even said, "I will satisfy her and hence have a better position in this house. After all God will forgive me when I repent." No! He was conscious of the consequences of sin- it destroys a person's relationship with God. Therefore, he stood firm and replied "how then can I do this great wickedness and sin against God?" His firmness thus is reflected in the manner in which he resisted the woman throughout his service in the house. In our world today, you stand the risk of facing the same temptation several times. If Joseph prayed to God and developed self-control, you can do the same and resist every temptation to the sin of sexual intercourse. I call that the Joseph's vow.

If you want to stand firm in the Lord and get a wonderful marriage, then you have to take the Joseph's vow of chastity today and ask for self-control and wait for the day of your marital blessing. If Joseph accepted the offer of free sex, he would have remained a slave in the house of Potiphar and risk execution when his master discovers him. He would have destroyed God's plan and destiny for his life. However, he took a vow. *"Lord I will never yield to the temptation of immorality. I prefer to run away half-naked than to destroy my relationship with you Lord."* God honoured his vow and though he was jailed, it was God's pathway to greatness. He rose from the marginal position of foreigner and became the Prime Minister of Egypt. He also married a beautiful lady and had two handsome sons, Manasseh and Ephraim. Exceptionally they became fathers of two tribes in Israel. Be a Joseph in your generation. Be a Mary, (Jesus' mother) who though was at the age of marriage had jealously guarded her virginity. If you are determined to take the Joseph's vow today, then pray this prayer from the depths of your heart.

"Lord Jesus, thank you for being my Lord and Saviour. I dedicate my body to you from today henceforth as your temple and I promise to keep it holy. I reject all sexual sins in all its manifestations. Today I take the Joseph's vow of chastity. I promise Lord that nobody will see my nakedness in the sexual sin. I promise to preserve my body and flee from all immorality. Lord grant me self-control from today so that whenever I am tempted, I will remember this day that I have set myself apart for you. Thank you Lord for hearing and answering me. In Jesus' name I pray. Amen"

CHAPTER 7
The Choice of a Life Partner

Amadou and Mildred in their excitement and optimism believed they could make it together as husband and wife. After a period of friendship, they sought spiritual counseling from their local pastor. The pastor prayerfully took them through several counseling sessions. Yet he advised them against marriage since they would not make a good match. They were, however, very positive about their choice and trusted that through faith in the Almighty God they would make it. Unfortunately, in less than two years of being together, their marriage hit the rocks.

Amadou, a Nigerian, who studied in Cameroon while living in the northern part of the country. While in school, he had received conversion through the student's ministry and made good progress in his faith. Though an architect and contractor by profession, he was generally lazy and slow, and could not make it in business because he disappointed most of his customers.

Mildred hailed from the southern part of Cameroon, of Bassa origin who was living in the North. As a frustrated school dropout, she worked her way into the oldest profession of the world – selling her body. Before she believed, she had committed an abortion, and was treated severally for sexually transmitted diseases. Though hot tempered, she is very hard working. As a believer, she had to adjust a great deal, learning to live below her previous standards, but the joy of her salvation kept her making remarkable progress. She was also a few years older than Amadou.

They got married despite the pastor's caution and it did not take long for many incompatibilities to surface. The going was tough and rough. Quarrels, disagreements, sexually transmissible diseases, sterility, misery, poverty, and even scuffles were part of their daily life. As these vices gradually gained a comfortable position in the home of this young couple, their Christian testimony became less and less apparent. Several times, I was in the panel of counselors, as the center of this union could no longer hold. I remember during one of the sessions, this young man despite all his shortcomings, kept quoting a verse of Scripture to drive home his decision to divorce. He hung on Proverbs 21:9: *"Better to live on a corner of the roof than share a house with a quarrelsome wife."*

Today these two fine Christians are living thousands of miles apart. Amadou escaped to Nigeria, but Mildred remained in the North. Mildred went through a tough period of depression, backsliding before making peace with God and receiving spiritual healing. She was traumatized by the experience that she opted to remain single for the rest of life. Nothing much is known about Amadou except for the fact that he soon contracted another marriage without divorcing his former wife. It is evident that his spiritual life must be non-existent.

The Bible says, *"He who finds a wife finds what is good and receives favor from the LORD (Proverbs 18:22)"* and *"May your fountain be blessed, and may you rejoice in the wife of your youth (Proverbs 5:18)"*. But this was not the case with Amadou and Mildred. We will see why it was not so as we discuss the criteria for the right choice of a life partner.

Three Biblical ways of choosing a life partner

A careful study of the Bible reveals three different ways practiced in the *Old Testament* for the choice a life partner.

1. **God chooses and the individual confirms.** This was the case with Adam and Eve in the Garden of Eden. Another example is that of the choice of Rebecca for Isaac by Eliezer the servant of Abraham after having received clear instructions from his master (*Genesis* 24). Isaac never knew Rebecca before. However, when they met, their hearts were knit together and his wife comforted Isaac since he had just lost his mother.

2. **The individual chooses and God confirms.** Jacob chose his wife and then God approved his choice. Though Laban had two daughters and Leah was the elder, Jacob loved Rachel the younger *"because she was lovely in form and beautiful" (Genesis 29:17)*. King David got married to Abigail the widow of Nabal. *"Then*

David sent and wooed Abigail, to make her his wife (1 Samuel 25:39). Samson also got a Philistine girl for a wife. He fell in love with this girl and pleaded with his parents, *"I have seen a Philistine woman in Timnah; now get her for me as my wife" (Judges 14:2).* The Bible further says in verse 4 *"this was from the Lord".* God will always confirm clearly any relationship that is of Him.

3. **Someone else makes the choice:** The choice is made either by parents or as reward of some great achievement. Joseph was given Asenath, the daughter of the priest of On as wife after he interpreted Pharaoh's dream. King Saul gave his daughter Michail as wife to David because he succeeded in killing 200 Philistines. Hagar got a wife for her son Ishmael without his consent. This method is still very common in many traditional African societies, but is not recommended because it is not based on love. This sort of marriage is more likely to fail, especially when God is not in it.

The first two methods are good and recommendable. They emphasize the truth of the presence of a trinity in marriage; the male, the female and God, and the three must agree. In the third example above, this tri-union is absent and it becomes dangerous because the consent of the two main actors is not sought. It is obvious, however, that the consent of parents is important and should always be considered. Nevertheless, parents should not choose a life partner for their offspring because the final consent should be between the two and their God.

Is everyone called to get married?

World statistics estimate the natural sex ratio at birth to be close to 1.06 males to female and the ratio between *15 to 64 years is* 1.02 males to female. However, these percentages vary from nation to nation and from region to region. But generally when we observe different spheres of society; the media, schools, church, and public manifestations, the tendency is that there are more female than men. The Bible however, emphasizes monogamy – one man to one woman. It is therefore obvious that not everybody can get married. The Bible makes us understand that some people are called to a life of celibacy. *"For some are eunuchs because they were born that way; others were made that way by men; and others have renounced marriage because of the kingdom of heaven. The one who can accept this should accept it" (Matthew 19:12).* Biblically, then, there are three kinds of Christians called to a life of celibacy. This passage calls them *Eunuchs.*

1. **Natural eunuchs:-** These are people who are born with a defect that makes it impossible for them have children. Some boys are born without testis and girls without a uterus, ovaries or a vagina. Such people are eunuchs by birth because they may never develop secondary sex characteristics and could never procreate. Such cases are, however, very rare medical findings. Some never know it until puberty. That is why parents are advised to have their children properly examined at birth by a pediatrician, or some other qualified medical staff because some cases could be remedied. For example, cases of non-descended testis could be handled surgically. If there were, no way out one would turn to God either for a miracle or for grace to accept the condition.

2. **Man-made eunuchs:-** They may result, either from disease, accidents, or imposed surgery. There are certain viral diseases like mumps that can destroy the testis or ovaries. The victim is usually unaware of this fact and may only discover it at puberty, or after marriage. Other diseases may include tumors or infections needing surgical ablation. Cases of accidents that destroy reproductive organs are well known in medicine. The last possibility here is that of the Ethiopian eunuch mentioned in Scripture. In the ancient days, and even up till the last century, in certain cultures the men who took care of the queen or some important women of influence were castrated in order to prevent the slightest possibility of sexual indiscretion. While castration made

them grow huge enough to be good bodyguards, they were sexually impotent.

3. **Eunuchs for Christ:-** This group concerns those who with all their sexually viable yet have dedicated their lives to the service of God. The apostle Paul was an example and he writes,

> *I would like you to be free from concern. An unmarried man is concerned about the Lord's affairs - how he can please the Lord. But a married man is concerned about the affairs of this world - how he can please his wife - and his interests are divided. An unmarried woman or virgin is concerned about the Lord's affairs: Her aim is to be devoted to the Lord in both body and spirit. But a married woman is concerned about the affairs of this world - how she can please her husband. I am saying this for your own good, not to restrict you, but that you may live in a right way in undivided devotion to the Lord. (1 Corinthians 7:32-35)*

This advice came from no other person but the chief of eunuchs for Christ.

It must, however, be emphasized here that the Bible makes it clear in chapter 19 of Matthew that only those who can accept this should do so. Paul also states in 1 Corinthians 7 that if anybody burns with sexual desire, he or she should get married. It is not at all to God's glory to pretend to be a eunuch for Christ and yet live a secret immoral life.

CHAPTER 8
Criteria for the Choice of a Life Partner

Every youth must consider several qualities for the choice of a life partner. Unfortunately, in the past, many young persons have jumped into marriage without making important considerations and the evidence is there, even in the Christian circles. Several Christian marriages are on the rocks. Even when the spouses dare to stay together, one discovers that their relationship is characterized by misunderstandings, quarrels and disappointments. Many Christian homes are far from being what God ever intended. It is therefore crucial that the unmarried should give careful thought to this issue before ever getting in. I am glad you are reading this book.

Some preachers and authors talk of **major** and **minor** qualities that one may look for in a partner. They advise that one can compromise the minor, but not the major qualities. We are taking a totally different approach here to enumerate a couple of qualities every youth must consider before marriage. We will end up by summarizing what we consider most important.

1. **A believer must get married only to another believer.** Eunice was misled by wrong counseling to get married to an unbeliever with the hope that he would be converted in the process. From the beginning, things seemed to go well and they had a baby boy. Then, as if hell was released against Eunice, the husband started to torment her severely asking her to choose between him and her God. He began drinking heavily, smoking and chasing other women. Eunice, however, stood firm in her faith while things became worse and worse until he finally kicked her out of his life. He never cared for a divorce procedure before getting married to another woman. *"After all,"* he said, *"I know she can never get married again except I gave her a divorce bill."* For twenty-five years that I have known Eunice, she has lived as a single Christian, his young son being her only human comfort. Several times I heard her regret bitterly for the wrong choice, but there is nothing she could do.

The Bible warns believers from getting married, or having intimate links with unbelievers. When Abraham wanted a wife for his son Isaac, he gave clear instructions to his servant Eliezer, *"I want you to swear by the LORD, the God of heaven and the God of earth, that you will not get a wife for my son from the daughters of the Canaanites, among whom I am living, but will go to my country and my own relatives and get a wife for my son Isaac." (Genesis 24: 3-4)* Saint Paul also cautions believers in 2 Corinthians 6: 14-17: *"Do not be yoked together with unbelievers. For what do righteousness and wickedness have in common? Or what fellowship can light have with darkness? What harmony is there between Christ and Belial? What does a believer have in common with an unbeliever? What agreement is there between the temple of God and idols? For we are the temple of the living God. As God has said: "I will live with them and walk among them, and I will be their God, and they will be my people." "Therefore come out from them and be separate, says the Lord. Touch no unclean thing, and I will receive you."* May the Spirit of God sow this in the heart of every unmarried believer; *"It is better to be patient and wait for God's timing than to be unequally yoked with an unbeliever in marriage."*

2. **Physical appearance.** Beauty is relative or subjective; however, your partner must be charming to you. Height, Form, Face, Size, Complexion, etc., are all qualities that one should look for. One must, however, remember that with age one's spouse would change in size and structure. For instance, most people would gain weight after marriage. Women in particular gain more weight with every other pregnancy. A fair way of forecasting what your partner would look like in later life is to see the physiognomy of the mother for girls and that of the father for boys. Most girls and boys tend to be like their mothers and fathers respectively in later life.

It must be made clear here that God never forces a partner on somebody. The person chosen must be to your taste. I remember the case of a young Christian leader whom

I asked why he had decided to get married to a particular emaciated girl weighing less than 50kgs. His response was, *"It is God's will. If not of God, I would never dream of getting married to a girl who is as skinny as a wasp."* I immediately told him to break the relationship because God would never force us against our will. He makes us willing by working in our inner man. Thank God he obeyed and today is happily married to someone else.

3. **Character and temperament.** These two important elements go together and influence one another. Rebecca, the wife of Isaac, was a hard working lady. She offered to give water to the Camels of Abraham's servant (Genesis 24: 18-20). One camel can drink more than 100 liters in a go. If she had to draw out water from the well for ten camels, then it demonstrates a spirit of a helpmate and a willingness to serve. David got married to Abigail because of her character (1 Samuel 25:18-31). She was wise; open-handed, outgoing, humble, and a fluent speaker.

Several years before marriage, I was interested in a beautiful and elegant sister, but a friend discouraged me. He said, *"Daniel, I know what you desire of a wife. Immaculate has one of the best physiognomies you could ever have for a wife, but you do not know her character. She is nonchalant, lazy, nagging, and strong-willed and above all cannot cook well. I know you like good food. She is not your match."* The writer of Proverbs says that a woman of noble character is worth far more than rubies and worthy to be praised (Proverbs 31:10).

4. **Compatibility.** This talks of the ability to blend. The two should understand, accept or tolerate each other. There are three areas of compatibility we want to underscore here.

- **Intellectual compatibility.** This concerns the levels of education, both formal and informal. There should not be a broad margin between the two persons because it would create problems of communication. One of the greatest problems in marriage is that of communication. When there are misunderstandings because of poor comprehension, it can result in complexes (superiority or inferiority complexes).

- **Cultural compatibility.** This problem is more felt in Africa than in Europe and America. Every African country has several tribes with different cultures and traditions. This poses a cultural compatibility problem in marriage. Behavioral patterns, food habits, dressing, customs, and language barriers are a few of the problems encountered. It is therefore advisable to be cautious about multi-cultural marriages. The experience in our country has been that marriages between Anglophone and Francophone or between blacks and whites have not been very successful. Though marriages between people of different tribes are becoming more and more commonplace, cultural incompatibility must always be taken into consideration.

- **Spiritual compatibility**. The Bible says that the woman is a helpmate fit for the man meaning that she is to be a helper, collaborator, companion and co-worker to accomplish God's purpose for the couple. There is therefore a necessity for similar passion and zeal for the work of the Lord. There must be spiritual agreement and vision. If only one person has a yearning to serve God, then there is incompatibility at this level.

Several years ago, I counseled two young Christians for marriage. The girl was burning with zeal to impact her generation for Christ. But the young man was satisfied to be a Christian and was just interested in maintaining a stable faith in Christ and making good monies. Today, their marriage is a bed of problems, frustrations and spiritual redundancy. They are materially rich, but spiritually poor. They are living in their own house, each of them drives a good car and they have 3 children, but the marriage is on the verge of breaking.

It would be presumptuous to think that one can see the spiritual pathway from the onset. God may reveal things one day at a time, but the need for compatibility in spiritual matters from the onset cannot be overemphasized. Aquila and Priscilla are good biblical examples of a couple that complemented one another spiritually.

5. **Complementary.** In marriage, the two persons would hardly be of the same temperament or have the same characteristics. The wife is expected to make up for the missing elements in the life of the husband, and vice versa. They are expected to complement one another. If one is lazy, the other should be hard working, if one is a spendthrift, the other should be careful, and if one is hot-tempered, the other should be a peacemaker, etc. Imagine a home where the two persons have an explosive temper; it could be very dangerous. On the other hand, if the both spouses are slow in taking decisions, many opportunities would be lost. It is vital to look for someone with whom you would be complementary.

6. **Background.** This is an area that most believers do not bother about, meanwhile it is of utmost importance. It may not prevent the marriage, but it would help one to watch out for certain setbacks that need to be settled before marriage.

   - **Family background.** It is necessary to know whether your partner is from a monogamous or polygamous family, a traditional or an enlightened one. There may be family traits or family linked diseases like sickle cell anemia, hemophilia, hypertension, diabetes, obesity; character associated flaws like prostitution, banditry, and drunkenness; or cases of family curses, including poverty, joblessness, abortions, premature deaths and marriage instability. All these factors should be scrutinized. It could even be that you might be getting involved with a family of witches and wizards. Never simply dismiss these issues by saying you are in Christ and nothing can happen to you. Other believers, including spiritual leaders, have been affected by their family background. You are no exception. If these conditions exist, appropriate measures must be taken for deliverance before the marriage takes place.

Evangelist Albert is a good friend of mine. When he had his first child, a beautiful daughter, after a few months of existence, he discovered that the child was abnormal. She was virtually a vegetable baby. She could not sit at four months, crawl at six, nor stand at one year. She was a non-developing mass of protein that only ate and increase in size. Despite all the medical attention, fasting and prayers, she passed away after close to two years of existence. This was a hard blow to a young couple and Albert did not take it lying down. He decided to take a retreat to wait on God to find out why. The Lord spoke to him clearly. There was a family curse that was at the root. God asked him to go find out from his father. His findings were astounding. Several years back, his parents and uncles, during a family sacrifice, had dedicated all the first-borns to an evil spirit. The consequences were that since then all the firstborns in the family died as babies. His case was therefore not exceptional and even though he had believed, he was not excluded from the curse that plagued the family lineage. After understanding this, he gathered all the believers in his family, explained this to them and they all prayed, breaking the curse. It is now more than two decades, all his younger brothers and sisters who got married after that have their first-borns alive and doing well.

In another case, a lady was engaged to a young man who had sponsored her in school; taken care of her and had already paid her bride price. Unfortunately, for this young man, the girl believed in Christ and so turned down the marriage proposal - and rightly so, given that he was an unbeliever. This young man, therefore, through a medium blocked the girl from ever getting married. Beautiful as she was, for the next ten years she could not find a suitor. During the visit of a prophet in her city, the Lord revealed these details to his servant. She was prayed for and advised to pay back the property of the unbeliever. Today, she is happily married to an anointed servant of God. Investigating the family background is important because it can bring out many hidden facts.

- **Personal past history:** It is advisable to open up to one another concerning your past lives. If there have been abortions, prostitution, previous venereal diseases, children out of wedlock or surgery; it is good to let your future partner know. Do not be afraid that these things may frustrate his love for you. If they do, then you were never meant to be together. The Bible says that perfect love casts out all fear. Also, in 1 Corinthians 13 it says that true love always protects, trusts, hopes and preserves. I know several cases of Christian marriages that have hit the rock because from the onset the past was hidden and was only discovered after marriage when certain previous damages could neither be repaired nor tolerated. The story of Mr. David and Juan is a case in point. Juan as an unbeliever lived a loose life had a son and an ectopic pregnancy that caused the removal of one of her tubes. In her fear that she may not be able to have a child again, she did an X-Ray examination of her remaining tube and it was confirmed that it was blocked. However, during courtship with David, she hid these facts and they got married only for David to be disappointed in waiting in vain for a pregnancy. Because of David's African background with pressure from the family, because of bitterness for having been tricked and the unquenchable desire for children, he was obliged against his faith to divorce and remarry. Needless to say that he is not more in Christ. Juan however, is continuing with her relationship with Christ as a singleton.
- **Family responsibility.** One needs to know if the person one is getting married to has family responsibilities or not. In Africa, the first son or daughter may receive all the necessary education because the parents are expecting him to then take care of the younger ones. It would be unfair to that family to get married to such a person and cut the financial link. Robert as a working

class university graduate was already taking care of his parents and younger ones. Then he gained a scholarship for post-graduate studies abroad. He did not only come back home with a Master's degree, but also with a beautiful white for a wife. Then tensions began to rise in their marriage because of the extended family parasites who flocked to their home without prior notice. These family members also were shocked at the reaction of Robert's traumatized white wife. The first few years of their marriage were really hurtful and it came almost to breaking point. A lot of prayer, counseling and adjustments had to be made. These hurts could have been avoided if proper preparation had taken place.

7. **Premarital medical records.**

Sara is a medical doctor with the sickle cell trait. Neglecting medical scrutiny, she got married to a man also with the sickle cell trait. They have spent their lives burying sickle cell children. On the other hand Rev. Bob fell in love with Pamela, a charmingly beautiful and apparently very healthy sister. Unfortunately, on medical screening she was discovered to have AIDS. Painful as it was, they broke their engagement. He got married much later on to another beautiful sister and they are happily serving the Lord today. Sister Pamela not long after this developed the full-blown disease and today is in glory. It would have been stupid for the pastor to get married by faith. Some believers contest this advice, but let us remember that as one preacher said *"love may be blind but marriage is an eye opener."* It is absolutely necessary to do some prenuptial medical tests, including, hemoglobin type and Rhesus factor, sexually transmissible diseases, AIDS test and viral hepatitis. The results of these tests could bring about three resolutions concerning the relationship. In case of a positive AIDS test, Sickle cell trait in both parties, and a terminal disease like cancer, we strongly disapprove of any marriage. In case of damaging effects of sexually transmittable diseases with little or no chances of pregnancy, or in case of other findings that may endanger the couple's happiness, we counsel the parties concerned to strongly reconsider their positions. The last case is when the findings can be treated or do not disfavor marital union.

Fabien believed when he was the vice-principal of a public secondary school. His life as a teacher had not been the best. He had gone out with all colors and shapes and had become a silent reservoir of a variety of bacteria strains. He got married to Margaret who was a virgin and shared generously with her his bacterial reserves. The consequences were obvious. Not only was she constantly sick, but there was no forthcoming pregnancy. Since she was the one suffering from the disease, she was the one constantly being treated only to be re-contaminated after the next sexual contact. The husband came to complain to me after two years of marriage. I did not only counsel him but also consulted him and gave treatment for both of them. Six months later on, I met him in town on a visit and he fell on my neck. *"Thank you very much brother for the treatment. My wife is four months pregnant,"* he exploded, hardly retaining his tears of appreciation. It is for your good to do this pre-marital medical check-up.

8. **The test of love.**

Love is a simple experience, but very difficult to define. However, when someone is in love, it becomes obvious both to the one in love and to the one that is loved. Quite often, the difficulty exists in differentiating between lust and love. We will come to that soon. 1 Corinthians 13: 4-8 describes the qualities of love:

> *"Love is patient, love is kind. It does not envy, it does not boast, it is not proud. It is not rude, it is not self-seeking, it is not easily angered, and it keeps no record of wrongs. Love does not delight in evil but rejoices with the truth. It always protects, always trusts, always hopes, and always perseveres. Love never fails."*

The question we want to answer here is how do I know that I love him or her with marital love? From our years of counseling experience, we propose here three personal evaluation tests of marital love: - the mathematical formula, the circumstantial question, and the love curve test.

a) The mathematical formula: Love is not mathematics, but there is a simple mathematical method of being sure that you have made the right choice. This formula answers the question *'Is she/he the best person in the world I would ever want to get married to?'* The point here is that each person has qualities that he/she is looking for a life partner. But let me tell you frankly that you would never meet a girl or boy that matches perfectly all the qualities you desire. Such qualities may include; age, size, tribal origin, height, level of education, race, character, food habits, spiritual standards and aspirations, ambition, family background and financial standing. It is impossible to always meet someone who will match all these expected qualities and more, but it is always possible to meet the best of all such persons who is meant to be your life partner. Let me use the school examination principle to let you understand the mathematical formula. When someone is declared first in class, it is neither because he scored 100% in all the subjects, nor because he was the best in all the subjects. He might be 3rd in mathematics, 2nd in English, 10th in French, 8th in chemistry, 1st in Biology, 5th in physics, etc. But when the sum total of his marks is made, he scores highest in that class. He is then proclaimed the best student. That is the mathematical formula. The girl or boy you want to get married to may not be the best qualified in education, character, shape, age and all the other qualities mentioned above. But when you put all these qualities together in one person, she/he scores best of all the persons you have met or would ever meet. That is most likely your life partner.

b) The circumstantial question: The Bible says that perfect love casts out all fear and can bear all things. The circumstantial question concerns variables in the life of one another and is a test of our unchanging commitment to an individual in the uncertain and varying circumstances of life. Here are three circumstantial questions.

- Without considering the fact that we are Christians would, I still have gone in for her/him? This question is important because it eliminates the element of God forcing his will on you. There is also the undesired possibility of one person backsliding after marriage.
- Do I love him/her enough to accept her/him with his/her weaknesses and failures? The Bible says that perfect love covers a *multitude* of sins. If I am not sure to be a protector, if there is the slightest tendency of an accuser or of an expositor of her/his weaknesses, then I am not really in for that person.
- Would I still love him/her in all changing circumstances of life? Circumstances in marriage and daily life are bound to change with time and not always for the better, but often for the worst. It may include joblessness, financial crises, sickness, sterility, and even backsliding. Would I still love, respect and care for the person if conditions get worse? Jack, a student pastor got married to charming Lauren. They enjoyed their marital life for barely two years and Lauren developed a debilitating disease that made her a helpless burden to take care of. Pastor Jack could neither enjoy sex, outings with his wife, nor have children. Some people advised him to divorce and remarry justifying their counsel by the fact that it was not his fault. But genuine love with godly fear kept Jack faithful for twenty three years of patient care and concern for his wife before she passed onto glory. No one can ever predict such a situation but it is part of the circumstantial question that determines genuine love.

c) The love curve test. Time is a good test of love. The modifications that take place with the love curve would determine whether it is true love or lust. Love is a **strong feeling of affection** for someone, but lust is a **strong sexual attraction**. There is a difference between the curve of true love and false love (lust in general). True love grows with time. As you get to know each other better your love interwoven and become stronger and is not destroyed by the knowledge of the weaknesses or failures of one another. But when doubts and uncertainty start invading your heart, unrest in your spirit or the love curve starts going down, then it is a serious warning. This is a sure proof that it was not genuine love from the onset. Something that can help during this period as you study one another is to observe the person's reaction in different circumstances – when provoked to anger, when faced with a problem, when in conflict with another person... Such circumstances would help in modifying positively or negatively the love curve in your heart.

Fig 8.1: **The love curve**

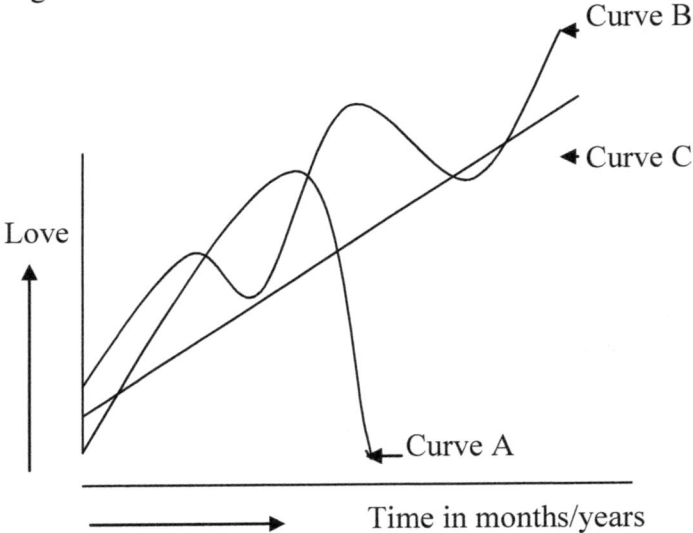

Curve A: This is a typical case of lust. It lasts for some time and then suddenly drops, especially after the young man has satisfied his sexual desires by luring the girl to bed.

Curve B: This is the case of genuine love, which has developed with time but through difficulties, maybe temperamental clashes, tensions, external influences etc.

Curve C: This is another case of genuine love that has encountered little or no major problems. This case is however more dangerous than B because they have not really known each other. There are bound to be hitches amongst two persons who come together from different backgrounds and with different experiences.

9. **What does God say?** Before taking a final decision about marriage you must hear God's voice. He must speak to you so clearly that there would be no doubt in your heart. Even though God can and does speak through dreams, visions, revelations or prophecy, I do not advise any of these ways when it comes to marriage. The reason is simple. Here, we are dealing with an emotional problem and it is very easy for your carnal sub-conscious man to build up any of these visual and verbal images that can be mistaken for God's voice. The best way to hear God's voice is through **His Word.** It is advisable at this moment to take a fasting retreat. Fasting breaks the external carnal flesh and renders your spirit sensitive to the Holy Spirit. A retreat takes you away from other activities and especially from physical contact with the person you love if you happen to be in the same town.

When God wants to speak to you through a passage, it is as if that passage literally jumps from the page of the Bible and sticks to your heart and you cannot shake it off. This would be accompanied by a personal internal conviction that gives you real certainty about your choice. There should be no pretense here because you would be the one to regret. There should be no marriage out of pity, pressure, or external factors like riches, position, gifts, spirituality, etc. This is a problem especially with girls. They get married to footballers, musicians, preachers, artists, and so on, because of their talents, but not to the man as a person. When the external factors that influenced the marriage wane or happen to disappear, the marriage crumbles. Only God's grace keeps such marriages going. This is one of the reasons why some marriages break even after several years and even after the birth of many children.

10. Accept the counseling of spiritual leaders and parents. We must understand that parents or counselors always have the best interest of the young people at heart. Their hesitation or denial is not a sign of hatred, lack of love or a blockage from their getting married. They are already married but want to genuinely help you to a better future.

Daniel and Grace loved each other and really wanted to get married. But each time they met their spiritual counselor, he would say something like this: *"Please, let's still wait and pray. I have had several cases like yours with some intellectual incompatibility, but I had peace in my mind to ask the persons to continue. But in your case, I have not yet received the green light from God."* These young people were living in another town and each time they afforded transport and came, he would simply give this kind of response. On the third occasion, the sister was so angry that when they went back she started questioning if this spiritual leader had even prayed about the situation. I believe now that he had received a NO from God and was playing for time so that these young people would discern God's will for themselves. I say so because shortly after the third incidence the brother lost his peace, took a fasting retreat and God spoke to him clearly that it was not His will. Today they are both happily married to different persons.

There may be few exceptions to the fact above. In exceptional circumstances, parents or maybe some unspiritual counselors may object to a relationship that is of God. If you happen to be in such a situation, then consult another counselor.

*****

To conclude this chapter, it is important to understand that most of the above points are not absolute pronouncements on marriage. They are merely guidelines to help you make the right choice. I would like, however, to insist on the three last points in the following diagram.

Fig 8.2: Combination of marital factors

```
┌─────────────────────────────────────────────┐
│ Love                                          │
│     +         │                               │
│ God's will    ├────────────►successful        │
│     +         │                               │
│ Counsellors/  │              marriage          │
│ Parents' consent                              │
└─────────────────────────────────────────────┘
```

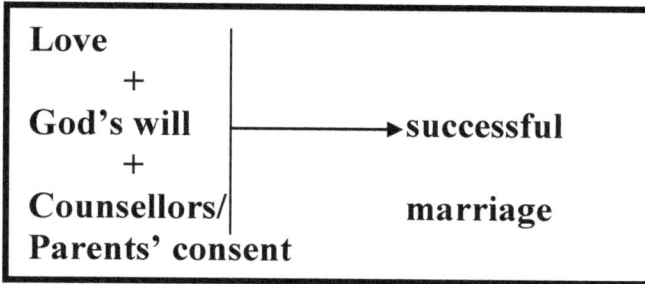

These last three criteria are essential for the following reasons.

- Love is the true bond of marriage. Marriage is built on love and nothing but love. When there is no genuine love, there is symbiosis but not marriage.

- God's confirming **will** for a union acts like an **anchor** in marriage. Even when marriage is in God's perfect will, there are still periods of hurricanes, tempests and brain-racking problems. It takes God's grace for two people from two different backgrounds with different characters, strengths and weaknesses to live together. It takes time to know and accept each other and finally to blend. During these moments of ups and downs, the affirmative word of God for the relationship serves as an anchor. More of this in the chapter on discerning God's will for a life partner.

- The advice of the mature (parents or counselors) who have had a wide range of experiences – though often ignored by young people is of utmost importance. The Bible says that in the multitude of counsel there is wisdom.

Heart-to-Heart Advice
1. **Be patient.** Tell the Lord you want to be patient and wait for his timing. The Bible says that there is a way that seems right in the eyes of a man, but the end thereof is destruction. Meanwhile those that wait upon and put their trust in the Lord will never be put to shame.
2. **Strive for excellence.** Tell the Lord you want your marriage to be an example to be emulated. God never hurries, and if He delays in answering your prayers, it is because He is still

polishing you up in all aspects of life - spiritual as well as physical so that before you marry you will be most prepared for your partner. Thank Him and continue to submit to His pruning process as He prepares you to become a model in your generation.

CHAPTER 9
Biblical Procedures of Marriage

The extended African family bonding makes it difficult for many people to live as a secluded immediate family. Many married young men are still so much under their parents' control that they receive instructions from them on how to manage their homes. It is even an accepted fact that the woman is the one who leaves her family to join the husband in their family. This fact is even portrayed in the change of name where the woman loses her family identity and takes on her husband's family name. These traditional facts and practices are totally different from biblical teaching. Genesis 2: 24 tells us that the man and the woman have to leave their families to cleave together in order to become one flesh.

*"Therefore shall a man **leave** his father and mother, and shall **cleave** unto his wife: and they shall become **one flesh**".* The Bible gives us three levels of marriage preparation or procedures;

- **Leaving**
- **Cleaving**
- **Becoming one.**

Let us try to understand what each of these procedures involves. The understanding may vary with cultures, but our explanation here is theologically based though with an African accent.

1. Leaving

There are two important facts hidden behind leaving. First of all leaving means *separation*. The two youths have to be detached from their families of origin in order to form a new family. This separation should be physical as well as spiritual. Physically they do not have to depend on their parents any longer for survival. This will be elaborated upon below. Spiritually, because quite often there are negative family foundations from which the young people have to separate. They need to prayerfully severe any negative spiritual links that could downplay their future and build a new family foundation on Jesus the eternal foundation that God laid. For more on this aspect, we refer you to our book entitled "Family Foundations; breaking generational curses and building positive family foundations."

Secondly leaving entails the ability to take care of a home. This capability is called *Maturity*. There are four kinds of maturity that make one fit for marriage. They are *physical, psychological, social,* and *spiritual maturity*. Let us see what each of them comprises.

a) Physical maturity

Physical maturity begins in boys when they can produce spermatozoids in a process called spermatogenesis. It is important for every young man to verify that both testes are in place because in some few cases the testes do not descend into the scrotum. In such a case a medical doctor should be consulted immediately. In girls, **oogenesis** results in the production of the ovum and this is externally demonstrated when they start menstruation. Physical maturity occurs well before one is fully prepared for marriage. God decided that this should be so, in order to teach us how to handle our sexual instincts long before marriage. Physical maturity takes place during the teenage years, between 9 and 14 years for girls and between 11 and 15 for boys. They begin to experience sexual emotions at this period and if they do not learn to exercise power over these emotions, they would end up becoming sexual perverts, prostituting to satisfy their sexual tensions. Sex was made for us and not us for sex. We are called to be the masters of our emotions and not the other way round.

Physical maturity also implies muscular strength that enables the person to work. A man who is physically mature is capable of hard work. In fact, the Bible admonishes that he who does not work should also not eat. We will say more about this when we come to social maturity.

b) Psychological (Mental) Maturity

Marriage is not just sex and pleasure. Marriage is more than that. It is *responsibility*. *Marriage is also being able to take decisions, solve problems, cater for others, dialogue with, and being able to sacrifice for the one you love.* All this refers to psychological maturity. A psychologically mature person considers the interest of others before his own personal interest.

A psychologically mature man is able to provide security at home by his reassuring presence. He is the head of the home and every member of his household looks up to him for care, concern, love and provision. He is the family vision caster. He should be able to plan for the family; project for the future and work towards it. This is only possible if he is mentally mature.

The woman must be able to take care of a home. This will involve cooking delicious meals or at least coordinating the kitchen activities, organizing the structural beauty of the home, including the parlor, rooms, and the surroundings, and being able to take care of children. *The weight of marriage dawns on the woman when after marriage she gets pregnant. While learning to cope with all the hormonal changes in her system, she still has to meet the needs of the husband, members of her household and continue with her job, if she is employed.* It takes mental maturity to manage all these activities.

c) Social Maturity

Social maturity refers to the ability to be socially responsible. Society has a lot of demands, the respect of societal norms and laws, the ability to act, react or interact in diverse situation, and, most important, the capability of providing for a family. As a young man, one usually has little or no weighty social responsibility. Youths usually have no financial obligations and few persons, if at all really look up to them. Getting married means one will not only take care of one's self, but also of a wife, a following and eventually children. You should be able to provide lodging, feeding, clothing, health facilities to those under your care. In fact, man is the source of the family's finances. This situation has been reversed or mismanaged in the African setting. In the village, it is the woman who does the clearing and farming, bears, delivers and caters for the children, takes care of the running of the home...

and the man is there just like a king without portfolio. Women's rights are blown out of proportion.

The Bible gives us God's stand point and it is important to understand that he is the author of marriage. After the fall of man, the curse upon the male states this; *"To Adam he said, "Because you listened to your wife and ate from the tree about which I commanded you, 'You must not eat of it,' "Cursed is the ground because of you;* **through painful toil you will eat of it all the days of your life. It will produce thorns and thistles for you, and you will eat the plants of the field. By the sweat of your brow you will eat your food** *until you return to the ground, since from it you were taken; for dust you are and to dust you will return"(Genesis 3:17-19 emphasis mine).* Man is the breadwinner of the home and must be socially mature to be able to do that. Be careful not to get married to a daydreamer, or one who builds castles in the air.

The woman, however, is called a helper. She is thus expected to help meet the needs of the family. Proverbs 31: 10ff describes a virtuous wife in these terms: "A wife of noble character who can find? She is worth far more than rubies. Her husband has full confidence in her and lacks nothing of value. She brings him good, not harm, all the days of her life. She selects wool and flax and works with eager hands. She is like the merchant ships, bringing her food from afar. She gets up while it is still dark; she provides food for her family and portions for her servant girls. She considers a field and buys it; out of her earnings she plants a vineyard. She sets about her work vigorously; her arms are strong for her tasks. She sees that her trading is profitable, and her lamp does not go out at night. In her hand she holds the distaff and grasps the spindle with her fingers. She opens her arms to the poor and extends her hands to the needy. When it snows, she has no fear for her household; for all of them are clothed in scarlet. She makes coverings for her bed; she is clothed in fine linen and purple. Her husband is respected at the city gate, where he takes his seat among the elders of the land. She makes linen garments and sells them, and supplies the merchants with sashes. She is clothed with strength and dignity; she can laugh at the days to come. She speaks with wisdom, and faithful instruction is on her tongue. She watches over the affairs of her household and does not eat the bread of idleness. Her children arise and call her blessed; her husband also and he praises her: "Many women do noble things, but you surpass them all." Charm is deceptive, and beauty is fleeting; but a woman who fears the LORD is to be praised. Give her the reward she has earned, and let her works bring her praise at the city gate."

Social maturity both for the boy and the girl is an essential quality for a good marriage. The man is the breadwinner and the woman is a helper made fit for him. They need to plan and realize projects together as the man spearheads.

d) Spiritual Maturity

Concerning spiritual responsibilities, the Bible says that the man is the head of the home and the woman a helpmate fit for him. Spiritual maturity here implies that the man has a sense of direction in spiritual matters. He should know where he is leading his family to. He is expected to be a role model, an example in word and deed. He should teach the family both theoretically and practically in matters of Christian virtues including, love, forgiveness, faith, honesty, prayers, conduct, and transparency. I do not advise young converts to get married. First of all they do not know how to discern God's will for their lives, how much more for a family. A spiritual man has a calling, a burden, and a plan of action. Here we are not talking of building castles in the air. Many young people are good at that, but a sensitive girl would easily discern such cases. A spiritual person would already have some spiritual fruit of his previous walk with God. The woman equally must be mature enough to know how to enhance her husband's calling.

In concluding this aspect of **leaving** the parents, the four types of maturity can be summarized as follows:

Physical maturity ⟶ the ability to procreate

Psychological maturity ⟶ the ability to handle responsibility

Social maturity $\longrightarrow$ the ability to meet family and social needs

Spiritual maturity $\longrightarrow$ the ability to develop a vision and lead the family to accomplish it

Table 9.1: Summary of maturity in boys and girls

Aspect of maturity	Boys	Girls
Physical	11 to 15 years	9 to 14 years
Psychological	21 to 24 years	18 to 21 years
Social	Be able to earn a living	Be able to support spouse
Spiritual	Spiritual vision and leader	Helper capable of enhancing husband's life and vision

2. Cleaving

Cleaving means bringing together, uniting two things to become one. This refers to the marriage procedure. In many nations, there are three levels of the marriage procedure, namely; Traditional marriage, Legal marriage and Christian marriage. The Bible recognizes the first two levels but the church has instituted the third and I believe God approves of it because it gives opportunity for the marrying to be blessed by the servants of God and the church. These three steps are therefore all important for a normal and lasting marriage. Let us look at these three steps.

a) Traditional marriage

This is the agreement between the two families. It is usually the most difficult part of the marriage procedure because Christians are often confronted with non-biblical traditional practices, which may include:

-Providing strong drinks and cigarettes;
-Pouring of libations;

-Offering sacrifices to idols and the gods of the family or the village;

-Subjecting the girl or the couple through demonic practices.

These practices vary from culture to culture, but all have the same origin; carnal pleasures of the extended families and appeasing the gods of the land. We need discernment to identify the practices that are demonic in order to firmly stand against them. This is why it is important to always go to the family with elderly spiritual leaders preferably from that locality or tribe because they are more conversant with the traditions and would know how to argue on your behalf, thus preventing you from falling into the devil's snare.

It is, however, necessary here to explain that not all traditional practices are evil. We therefore have to be careful not to unnecessarily complicate the traditional marriage. In some cases, in order not to prolong the traditional procedures, we advise that everything should be settled financially which the families can redeploy as they deem necessary.

b) Legal marriage

This is the procedure before the government officials. Your marriage is registered and you are recognized by the State as husband and wife. You are then given a marriage certificate. This is a step that many Christians neglect especially the uneducated. The Bible admonishes believers to be law-abiding citizens. "Everyone must submit himself to the governing authorities, for there is no authority except that which God has established. The authorities that exist have been established by God. Consequently, he who rebels against the authority is rebelling against what God has instituted, and those who do so will bring judgment on themselves. For rulers hold no terror for those who do right, but for those who do wrong. Do you want to be free from fear of the one in authority? Then do what is right and he will commend you. (Romans 13: 1-3)"

We therefore should make sure to have a marriage certificate before further procedures. This is extremely important for the sisters because whenever a relationship breaks they suffer more. I received in my office a sister who has been living martially with a man for 14 years and has had five children with him. But a few weeks before she met me, she was thrown out of the matrimonial home even while sick. The children had been bundled and sent to the village to fend for themselves and this man has taken a younger woman for a wife and has legalised a marriage with her. The former wife is now in the streets struggling for survival, separated from her children who are starving in the husband's village. Because of the prayers of this sister, this man during the 14 years of marital relationship was greatly blessed in his business. He built four houses, three in town and one in the village. Now while another woman is enjoying the fruits of her efforts and prayers, she is loafing without a habitat. Can you imagine such wickedness! Yet it exists and for those who do not heed to warnings. You have been warned. To be forewarned is to be forearmed. After signing the marriage legally, it is advisable that every party should keep his copy of the certificate.

c) The church blessing

This is purely a Church tradition that could vary from place to place, but there is so much spiritual importance attached to it. This ceremony is the moment when the Church approves of the marriage and the leaders lay their hands on the couple to invoke God's blessing. We do not see this practice in the Old Testament, but the New Testament gives us a picture of it through the parables of the marriage feast. The marriage of Jesus to the Church, His bride as explained in Revelation, is another example. Do not neglect the laying on of hands by the leaders to impart the blessings of God. Saint Paul advises Timothy, "Do not neglect your gift, which was given you through a prophetic message when the body of elders laid their hands on you" (1 Timothy 4:14).

God blesses that which is according to His will and which has been kept pure. God does not bless sin. The Bible says the marriage bed must be kept pure and undefiled, for God will judge all adulterers and the sexually pervert (Hebrews 13:4). We will see this more in the next section.

3. Becoming one

Becoming one in marriage involves both the sexual union and the children that result from this body union. The sexual act is the most intimate union than can ever exist between a man and a woman. Watch out for the chronological order of leaving, cleaving and becoming one. God is very methodical and orderly. *Biblically, sexual union is only allowed after the leaving and cleaving steps.* Any sexual union before the Church blessing is a sin and can only invite a curse on your marriage. I know many Christians who lived in sin before the Church blessing, but lied to the servants of God that they had not known each other sexually. All the marriages I know that started that way are either on the rock or are facing real tough times, except the one that I will recount to you. It is the case of a brother in one of the churches I co-pastored. The two persons knew themselves sexually and hid it from us. The Pastor who blessed the couple did not take the pains to find out if they had known each other sexually prior to the blessing. The marriage ceremony was not the best because there were lots of misunderstandings and disagreements, but the worst was yet to come. The first several months of the marriage were a hell on earth - quarrelling, fighting, bitterness, resentment and above all backsliding for both of them. The Pastor and I fasted and prayed for them because this brother was the only prominent indigenous believer in the church whom we thought would eventually take the lead if we both were to leave that town. One afternoon as we yearned before God for this couple, the Lord told us that they were haunted by their sin. We thanked God and moved straight to their home to confront them. After all they had suffered; they¹ could no longer pretend but conceded immediately. We had to lead them to confess their sin publicly before the whole Church. I can remember how they wept bitterly before the whole Church – and the Church members joined them in their tears. You know how those kinds of emotions can be contagious. We invited the Christians to forgive them, and then we laid our hands on them and prayed. That was the day of God's real blessing. Before that day, they had done everything to have a pregnancy, but to no avail. But as the sister testified later on, after that day, she never saw her menses again. God did not only forgive and heal their marriage, but also reopened her womb. Today, they have five children and are waxing strong in the Lord. I praise God for them because they humbled themselves. All the others I know, that pretended and played hypocrisy are reaping the results today. I do not know how to warn you enough. Please BE CAREFUL!!

Sin will destroy your marriage.
This is the moment to take a commitment before the Lord. If you have never had a sexual contact before now, then you are both a natural and spiritual virgin. But if you had sexual contact in the world before believing, God has forgiven the past and sees you today as a spiritual virgin. You are God's virgin. If you have already fallen into the sexual sin after believing, then repent sincerely before God and let the blood of Christ cleanse you of all sin. Take a vow of virginity today. Tell the Lord that no person will see your privacy in a sexual relationship before you are blessed in Church. Not even your fiancée, not even a day or the evening before your marriage. **Keep your virginity as a precious gem before God and only open up to your husband or wife after the church blessing.** The Bible sternly reminds us of this, "All other sins a man commits are outside his body, but he who sins sexually sins against his own body. Do you not know that your body is a temple of the Holy Spirit, who is in you, whom you have received from God? You are not your own; you were bought at a price. Therefore, honor God with your body" (1 Corinthians. 6:18-19).
I must also emphasize here that if there is a case of sexual sin, I blame the sisters more. This because a man is sexually excited by sight, but a woman is by touch. If the sisters restrain themselves from the wandering hands of brothers they would do themselves and these brothers a lot of good. A sexual relationship is only consummated when the woman yields to the man's desire. In the extreme case of rape, the Bible requires that the women should shout out for help. However, we know that in most cases of sexual sin, it is an agreement between the two

persons. **Please save your marriage by remaining pure and patiently waiting for the right moment.**

Commitment of virginity

> «*Lord I commit myself to a life of sexual purity and holiness before you. I promise to keep my virginity and pray that you O Lord will grant me victory over all temptations. Grant me the grace to be patient and wait for the partner that you have reserved for me. I pray this prayer of commitment sealing it with the blood of Jesus Christ. Amen*"

CHAPTER 10
Discerning God's Will for a Life Partner

"How can I really be sure that it is God's will for me to marry him/her?" This question is recurrent in most of our seminars and during pre-marital counseling sessions. It is the most crucial question to answer in matters of marriage. Apart from accepting Christ as Lord and savior, determining whom to marry is the next most important decision in life. Marriage as ordained by God is expected to be a heaven on earth but once you make the wrong choice, you also opt for a hell on earth.

Even when God ordains a marriage, there are always trying moments that can cause some momentary regret or provoke one to lose one's self-control and say some regrettable things. For instance, I know of a committed Christian once, out of anger, said to his beautiful wife, "I regret having gotten married to you." He later on repented, but the words still had serious negative repercussions. Such words can only come out of the mouth of someone who never had a clear word from God that God ordained his marriage. On the contrary, I happened to have lived with someone who had it rough at home, but he told me, "My marriage has kept going because I had a clear word from the Lord that Julian is my wife. If this were not the case, brother, I tell you we would not have been together today." So you see how important it is to hear clearly from God.

I always tell the young fiancés I counsel for marriage that a clear word from God about your life partner is an *anchor*. An anchor is a heavy metal usually shaped like a cross with curved arms which when dropped from a boat would grip the sea bedrock to prevent it from being tossed away by any violent waves or tempest. It is a security, a safeguard, and a custodian. That is exactly what the assurance of God's will do to a marriage. Every marriage has turbulent periods, tempests, and hurricanes. Even those of genuine believers too and such moments can be very serious and threatening. During those trials, the clear approval of God serves as the anchor to prevent your marriage from shipwreck. *Remember that you need that anchor before any further marital arrangements.*

Fig 10.1: An anchor

An anchor is a device normally made of metal, that is used to connect a vessel to the bed of a body of water to prevent the craft from drifting due to wind or current. A clear word from God serves as an anchor in times of crises, doubts, trials or pain. Let God speak clearly to you before you proceed in any marital relationship

Discerning God's will

It can be very difficult to discern God's will when it concerns the issue of marriage. This is because there is a strong emotional drive experienced by the lovers, which interferes with their ability to discern God's voice. Following are some guidelines to help you in discerning the voice of God.

1. Common Sense:

God has given us a mind and the ability to reason and take decisions. But many people want to put aside this natural ability that God has given them and prefer to hear voices from heaven. Each of us is endow with an intellectual quotient, which develops depending on our exposure, environment, and age. There are certain things that appear clear to our ordinary minds for which you do not even need to pray or seek God. With few exceptions, seeking God's will in prayer only comes in when natural reason has no clear solution to the problem. Moreover, for every believer, the Bible says we have the mind of Christ. For instance, you do not need to pray whether you should come out of bed in the morning or not, whether you should go to work or not. These are chores your common sense tells you to do. Concerning marriage, let us look at some examples. You do not need a voice from heaven to tell you not to get married to an unbeliever, or to a declared AIDS victim. Exceptions may be seropositive cases under control. Another example is if you have the sickle cell disease (homozygote drepanocytosis with SS hemoglobin), you also do not need God to tell you not to get married to another sickle cell patient, or even a sickle cell trait carrier (AS). Sickle cell patient is very rampant Africa. Sickle cell children are a real problem to their parents. They are regularly sick and many die young. So you see, there are certain decisions that are clear as we just reason them out. As Christians, we need to renew in our minds so that the Spirit of God will direct our reasoning. That is why the Bible says, "Do not conform any longer to the pattern of this world, but be transformed by the renewing of your mind. Then you will be able to test and approve what God's will is -- his good, pleasing and perfect will" (Romans 12:2).

2. Learning to hear God's voice.

There are three kinds of voices that we hear often. The first voice is that of the flesh. This voice is expressed through our emotions. What we see, hear, touch, smell, and feel affects our minds, which is the center of emotions. Our minds then react to these external influences by stimulating our appetites. It may be appetite for food, drink, sex, love, journey, and worship... depending on what was the stimulus. That is why the world uses advertisement as a powerful tool in marketing. Let us apply this in marriage. By regularly seeing a beautiful sister or a handsome brother, by inhaling the sweet fragrance of his or her perfume, by listening to her charming voice or his eloquent preaching, we can become emotionally attracted to the person. You may even dream about the person, or see visions. All this is just the voice of the flesh and nothing else. God has not spoken. Your emotions are sending out the message. A true story that has repeated itself so often is illustrative. A sister was in love with a handsome educated brother who was also a minister of the gospel. Each time this brother was ministering or was around, she was as if in trance, just dreaming of when she would be in his company. All her emotions were aroused. In her prayers she would see this brother before her, in her dreams she was with him, in fact, he was all over her mind. She could not imagine not ever living without this brother. This was purely the voice of the flesh, thus such a union could never be.

The second voice is that of Satan. It is quite different from that of the flesh. It may have to do with emotions but not always. In this case, the emotions would be influenced by demonic powers and they are strong and domineering. It may come as prophecy, a strong conviction, or voices that you hear in your mind, which could even be audible. Angela heard a clear voice when she was praying saying that Donald was going to be her husband. It came to confirm the interest that was already growing in her heart for him. Donald's caring and loving attitude to her as well as to other sisters around her had particularly won her heart. So this prophetic voice came as a confirmation. She decides to have a luring attitude towards Donald and if not of God's grace, the two would have fallen in the sin of fornication. It is only later on that it became known that Angela was possessed and the demons in her often gave her deceitful prophetic messages. When she was delivered she realized that marriage between them was not possible.

Lastly, and most important, is the voice of God. God speaks in diverse ways and we will be seeing that later on. Meanwhile, for one to learn to discern God's voice there is a need to be very close to the Lord. The following guidelines will help you.

a) Make it a practice to study the word of God. Those who get their minds soaked by the word of God will find it easier to know when God is talking to them because God never contradicts his word. But if you do not even know his word, then there is no common base for a conversation with Him.

b) Praying must be a two way process, a conversation, and not just a monologue. Many believers just go into God's presence to pour out their hearts to him and once this is done they are also done with prayer. This is not real prayer. We have to learn to listen to God and this implies that we have to learn to be quiet before Him. Learn to develop internal calm in our spirits in order to discern when he speaks. Tony Campolo, a popular American sociologist and minister to student groups, says we often have to be silent in God's presence for dozen of minutes and have our minds set on him before we can begin to hear Him.

c) Fasting is a strong means of listening to God's voice. When the flesh is an obstacle, we need to fast and break the outer man so that the inner man is set free. When our outer man is wasting in fasting, our inner man is being renewed in the nature of God and we become more sensitive to God's voice.

d) Practice makes perfect. No one is an expert in hearing God's voice. You have to be ready to act on what you think you have discerned as God's voice and let him confirm or disconfirm. We all learn by making mistakes and not anyone who takes no action because he is afraid to make mistakes would ever learn. Act on the convictions you receive in your mind after prayer and see the results. With time, you will be able to differentiate the convictions that are of the Holy Spirit and those that are not. God leads those who are ready to step out in faith.

3. Discerning God's voice through the word

I personally think this is the best way of discerning God's voice. God speaks through his word in several ways. The most important are as follows:

a) Directly through a verse, chapter or an event in Scripture. As you get aside to pray and study the word, you come across some Scriptures that speak into your situation. Don was in love with Grace and wanted to discern God's voice, so he took aside a fasting prayer retreat expecting the Lord to speak to him before he could break his fast. By the third night, he had not yet received a word from God, so he decided to continue praying and reading his Bible intermittently until God speaks to him. At about 2 am, he came through a passage that touched him. As he explains in his testimony, the passage seemed to have jumped out of the Bible to cling unto his heart. This was the passage; "Ephraim's glory will fly away like a bird-- no birth, no pregnancy, no conception. Even if they rear children, I will bereave them of every one. Woe to them when I turn away from them! I have seen Ephraim, like Tyre, planted in a pleasant place. But Ephraim will bring out their children to the slayer."

Give them, O LORD-- what will you give them? Give them wombs that miscarry and breasts that are dry. Because of all their wickedness in Gilgal, I hated them there. Because of their sinful deeds, I will drive them out of my house. I will no longer love them; all their leaders are rebellious" (Hosea 9:11-15).

These verses were written for the Israelites but as Don testified, "It was as if they left the page of the Bible and stuck to my heart. If they were a confirmation, I would have rejoiced over it. But they were verses that showed God's disapproval to my relationship with Grace and I understood why. I am a Sickle cell carrier and Grace happened to be one also. So the verses meant everything to me." Since Don was a man who desired God's best for his live, painful as it was, he had to break the relationship. God speaks clearly through the verses of Scripture especially when it comes to the issue of marriage.

b) God can bring to remembrance a verse of Scripture that was stored up in your sub-conscious mind. You know our minds are like the memory of a computer. When we read or study God's word, the hard disc of our brain stores up the information we have read. Then when there is a need, the Holy Spirit goes into your hard disc and looks for the appropriate verse that would meet that need. That is why the Bible says, "Let the word of God dwell in you richly." (Colossians 3:16). In other words, the Bible is asking you and me to stock the hard disc of our brains with the word of God so that when the Holy Spirit gets into it in time of need, it should not be empty. In one case of premarital counseling, I asked Mary to go and pray for God's confirmation. After some weeks, she came back excitedly and told me that the Lord had spoken to her. While she was fasting, praying, and seeking God's face, the Lord brought into her mind the picture of Rachel being taken to Isaac who was in the fields meditating. Simultaneously and vividly, these words of Scripture appeared in her mind, "He brought me to his banqueting house, and his banner over me is love. (SS 2:4). This was not just the imagination of her mind or worked up by her emotions, it was a confirmation from the Lord.

c) The Lord may speak to you through the spoken, written, or preached word. While you are praying and seeking God, He may use a preaching, a recorded message, a book, or any other form of the word of God to speak to you. God uses this way lot of times to speak into our lives. The following example does not concern marriage but it illustrates the point. Once I was going through a tough time in my life when my wife had been unjustly maltreated and was undergoing severe torture. I had developed great bitterness in my heart against her persecutors and was seriously thinking of revenge. Then one morning as I drove to work I carelessly picked up an apparently old cassette that had been lying around and decided to listen to the music that was on it. Fortunately, for me it was not music but a message entitled, "Should I still forgive him?" I tell you it was a powerful message God had placed on my way to speak forgiveness into my life. Before the message finished, I was weeping and praying for God to forgive me of a wicked heart and to grant me a forgiving spirit for those against whom I had developed bitterness in my heart.

4. Hearing God's voice through the Holy Spirit

Many believers as explained above have to train their spirits to be sensitive to the inner voice of the Holy Spirit. This is important because many times He will speak to us through the inner man. He does it either by flooding our inner man with peace and joy, or with unrest and irritability. In this case, of the inner witness, it is important that the person have a righteous relationship with the Lord.

Joseph had been maintaining a relationship with Josephine for several months and both were expecting their spiritual leaders to give them green light to start the traditional marital arrangements. But strangely enough their spiritual leader kept delaying telling them he had not yet had a clear word from God concerning their relationship. Then suddenly one afternoon, Joseph lost his inner peace but did not quite understand why. As his mind wondered from one idea to another, it finally settled on his relationship with Josephine and he realized that was the cause of his unrest. As he went aside to fast and pray about that relationship, the Lord clearly showed him that it was not in His perfect will for them to be married.

The Holy Spirit may also speak to us through an apparently audible voice, which may be heard by others or only by the concerned. That is what happened to Saint Paul on the road to Damascus. The Holy Spirit spoke to him in an audible voice that was heard also by those travelling with him (Acts 9: 7). God has not changed. He still does the same today. Elizabeth's testimony illustrates the point. She stood up one morning to have her meditation and as she was praying, she heard a clear audible voice that said "No, No, No!" And that was all. She wondered who had entered her room that early morning with the door still locked. She asked who it was, but had no answer. She then stood up and looked around, both within and without the room and there was absolute quiet that early morning hour. Not understanding what had happened she went back to prayer and finished her morning meditation. That same day, Flevous came around to visit her and on her way to see him off, he asked her hand in marriage. As Elizabeth explains in her testimony, "Before I could recollect myself to understand what was happening, the same words of the morning had come out of my mouth, 'No, No, No!' And then it downed on me that it was a for-message the Holy Spirit had given me, knowing what was going to happen that day." As she testifies, Flevous treated her for being carnal, but she had absolute peace because she knew God was in control. Learn to be sensitive to the voice of the Spirit of God in you,

4. God's voice through circumstances

God can and does speak through diverse circumstances. They may be experiences or counseling. When we encounter several obstacles on our way it is often necessary to review whether we are really on the right path. They may be put there by God or Satan, but whatever the case it is a word of caution. In one of the cases that I counseled, Gaby was in love with a sweet beautiful sister and was very positive about the relationship. But in my prayers and counseling I discerned it was not God's will. However, I did not tell him but kept encouraging him to go seek the Lord. He even got angry with me because I could not give him the go ahead. As time went on he realized that the two of them could really not make it as husband and wife and finally gave up the relationship. Today Gaby is happily married to another sister.

5. **Other methods of discerning God's voice**

There are several other methods of discerning God's voice including, prophesies, dreams, visions, laying of a fleece before God like Gideon, casting of lots etc. I kept these at the end because I want to sound a clear word of caution here. Indeed God speaks through all these methods and we have clear biblical examples, but when it comes to marriage it is absolutely not advisable to depend on such methods. This is because they can be highly influenced by self or by our emotions. For instance it is easy to dream about the brother or sister whom you love but that would just be a continuous functioning of your sub-conscious mind while you sleep. We have also had cases of false prophecies involving marriage. Lastly, laying of fleece and casting of lots are not biblically encouraged today with the advent of the Holy Spirit.

To conclude this important chapter, you must get a clear word from the Lord confirming your marriage engagement. This is why pre-marital counseling is of utmost importance because counselors would help you discern God's will for your life. Marriage counselors do not tell you God's will. They help you to find it out for yourself; at least that is what I do. Remember, of all the different methods given above, that of the written Word of God is incontestable. God watches over His word to confirm it and when you earnestly seek His face humbling yourself' in fasting and prayer, He would not disappoint you. Taking the decision of whom to get married to, would determine whether you would live a heaven or hell on earth. Therefore be wise.

CHAPTER 11
Courtship

The courtship period sets off when two persons agree to be married to the actual nuptials. It is an important period for the two persons because they can use it to prepare and plan, but it is a very dangerous moment because they get close to one another and the temptation to fall in the sin of premarital sex is very high. In many Christian settings, the approval of the leaders is important before the two can declare themselves fiancés. It is also advisable for it to be officially announced in Church so that other young people should not be tempted to sin thinking that their relationship is illegal. It also permits church and civil authorities to be certain that none of the persons has been married before or engaged to someone else. I strongly recommend that this period should not be long because of the exposure to temptation. We will examine what this period necessitates. We would end by giving advice to prevent the two from falling in sin or becoming an obstacle to other young people in Church.

What to do during this period
1. Get to know each other better.
It is a period of opening up to one another, of sharing and manifesting love practically. We propose that the following things should be shared.
- *Let the other person know in details who you are*. Learn to be sincere with one another and open up. Share about your past life including, family and upbringing, studies and friendships at school, likes and dislikes, hobbies and commitments, etc. It is not a time to pretend, hide your claws and fake how faithful and wonderful you are. It is also important to let the other person know about any family responsibilities and any past sexual experiences you have had. This is necessary because it would guide you for the appropriate medical check-up and would prevent any future guilt because you had hidden something from your partner.

- *Get to know the two families*. It is a moment for each of you to get close to the different members of both families. This is crucial especially in the African setting where family ties are quite strong. We have had in the past where young people got married without knowing either the villages of one another or the parents. This is an attitude that can cause strain in the future because some relatives can be very good at provoking crises.
- *Develop camaraderie.* You would get to understand eventually that your best friend is no longer some other person but your future spouse. Friends love to be together, share gifts and go visiting. It is a time to show the *Phileo* kind of love to your spouse – brotherly affection. Holding hands and going for a stroll, going window-shopping, visiting interesting sites and people. These are all activities that reinforce your camaraderie.
- *Show concern and interest to one another*. Look for opportunities to show concern and practical love. For the boy, it may be inviting your fiancée for a meal in a restaurant, taking care of some of her needs, take her out to entertainment programs, or buying her an engagement ring. This is not obligatory in the African background but an inescapable step in the Western world. The young man would usually surprise the girl during an outing in a park, in a restaurant or in some picturesque environment. This step is usually considered the official proposal of the boy.

For the girl, she may invite him for a home-prepared meal, surprise him with small presents, send him encouraging mails in times of stress etc. It is really a moment of developing and manifesting the love you have for one another.

2. Get your medical records clear.

We mentioned this earlier but this is the right moment to complete the list of prenuptial medical tests. We recommend medical tests under two groups, the obligatory and the facultative.

- *The obligatory medical tests.* If these tests are not done, they can jeopardize the future of the family. The first test is the HIV eliminatory test. AIDS has become very rampart even among Christians because some of the youths contacted it before believing. In Africa, Sickle cell anemia is very rampant also. We therefore insist that Hemoglobin electrophoresis is obligatory if the person's hemoglobin factor is unknown. The third compulsory test is blood grouping including the Rhesus factor. This third test does not really prevent marriage but it prepares the couple for any blood transfusion eventualities after accidents or during pregnancy. Tests for other sexually transmissible diseases fall under this group for those who have a past record of sexual activity. It is beyond the scope of this book to go into details but the Medical Doctors would usually explain to the concerned.
- *Facultative medical tests.* For those who are capable and understanding, it is good to make a complete check-up including, test for viral hepatitis, other laboratory tests for the blood, kidneys, a physical examination of the genitals and other paramedical examinations like ultrasound. Among those that we counseled we realized that some young ladies got married with large fibroids that were not identified, while some men had problems with undescended testis. Some of these couples have suffered from infertility and in Africa; this can often be very frustrating.

3. A time for planning

It is not easy for two persons who have lived apart and in different environments for decades to come together and live harmoniously without sitting together to plan. This is one of the main things that fiancés should do. Below are some of the areas to consider while planning:
- *Plan your future together.* They should discuss issues such as how many children they would love to have by God's grace, and where they would love to settle. Emmanuel is the only son to his parents and so they have inculcated in him

the idea that through him they would build a large family. Emmanuel wants to have as many children as possible. On the other hand, his wife Eunice comes from a large family and having observed the many traumatic deliveries the mother had, she is determined to have only two children. Then they got married without discussing this crucial issue. After their second baby, Emmanuel was shocked to his bones when his wife proposed that they should stop. This created a real hassle in their home until their pastor came in to resolve the problem. This is very common in most African settings. In the Western world though, there is a growing tendency towards having less children as many couples consider children a necessary ill. Moreover, many think it is difficult raising children and so the fewer they have the better.

Fortunately, for my wife and me, we considered this point seriously before marriage. I am the seventh of a family of nine and I thought my wife and I would have at least seven offspring. After all, if my mother did not have up to seven children she would not have had me as a husband. My wife on her part wanted two, at most three. Therefore, this was a cause of disagreement during our courtship. We, however, had to strike a balance and agreed on four. In the course of our marital life, she had three miscarriages and three difficult deliveries. In fact, God had to intervene several times to prevent a surgical procedure. As a result, we resolved to stop at three and she took on a safe contraceptive method. Nevertheless, somewhere along the line, she missed her period and on examination, it was discovered that she was pregnant again. In our fright, we asked God why he permitted it again despite our precautions. The Lord replied, "You forgot that during your courtship you asked me for four children? Yes you did forget, but I registered your prayer request. This is the fourth baby." And the Lord gave us a handsome second boy who is the center of interest in our home. We have a faithful God who remembers and answers our prayers in advance even when we ourselves forget. To Him alone be all the glory.

- *Plan how to manage your finances.* Determine whether both of you are picking up jobs or only one, and how you would manage your financial resources. There are three possible ways of handling family finances. The first way is to have a joint account and to have equal rights over the account. If both have a salary, the money comes into this account and the both manage it. The advantage here is that even when one person is not around, the other is not financially blocked. The disadvantage is that if one person were a spendthrift, he would squander family savings. The second possibility is that both of you own different accounts, but treat your finances together in one budget. You may want to create a third account that is a family account to which both of you have access but strictly under control. The third possibility is that each person has his account and manages it personally. However, in this case family responsibilities are shared as each person has specific things to do for the family. This gives a certain margin of liberty to one and the other. This is, however, possible only when the two persons have salaries. In case only the husband earns a salary the family budget must be one and the woman must not be treated like a slave or house girl. It is her right to have an allowance and it is necessary to emphasize that the allowance of the woman should be more than that of the man because they usually have more personal needs than the men do. I have had all kind of experiences with families that I have counseled concerning financial problems. In one case the woman who had no income confided, "He treats me virtually like a house girl. He gives me no pocket money and yet when he gives me food money, he wants me to give him an account of expenditure to the last franc I just feel like quitting." In another case the husband blurted, 'What does she need pocket money for? We draw up the market list together and whatever she needs can always be included in that list." In no way am I being the advocate of women, every man needs to understand that a woman with an empty purse feels very insecure and if the husband does not understand this can be a big source of frustration. Apart from the problems of sex and intimacy, financial upheavals is a real sore point in most homes around the world, and we say this after having done studies on it.

In our marital experience, we started with a one account and one budget management system but with time, we had so many difficulties because usually during the last week of the month we had serious financial crises. We finally decided to try the third option where each of us manages his/her account while having some responsibilities towards the family needs. Each of us has some financial liberty and can make surprise gifts to each other. We also have a family account to which both of us are signatories and none of us can get into the account except by common accord.

The last aspect about finances is budgeting. Many people need to understand the difference between functioning and investment budgets. The functioning budget is what is used to pay the bills, rents, food, telephone, electricity, water, medical insurance etc. But an investment budget is that which is put aside for investment or for the future – buy a plot, build, send the children to school, begin an income generating business etc. A person, family, church, nation that has no investment budget has no future. A few days ago, a young lady with already two kids came to my office and in the course of our conversation complained bitterly about the short-sightedness of her husband. He is the only breadwinner and for the four years they have been married she has tried to no avail to convince her husband about investing. She has even learned a trade and desired to start a small business, but her husband is neither willing to save towards it nor to take a loan for them to start the project. All that he earns is spent to pay bills and nothing more.

Courtship is the best moment to talk about these things. You may not really get to details because circumstances change with time, but at least financial management must have been evoked and possible management principles discussed.

- Plan your marriage feast. Some people like loud wedding feasts while others desire a quiet event. The lovers' opinions may differ. Courtship is a good time to sort this out. You also need to discuss issues like, those who are to be involved in the organization apart from family members, those to invite, where and how the ceremony would take place, who will be the ministers of the day etc. These are issues that are often neglected either because of lack of counseling, foresight, ignorance or just negligence. A divorce procedure for some couples begins on the day of marriage because hearts are torn apart with vexation, disagreements, or simple misunderstandings. Many of these problems would not arise if the courtship period were properly utilized to discuss them.

4. Time for fasting and praying together

Courtship is the time to build your marriage foundation by fasting and prayer. You can either make or mar your marriage during this period. If you take this time to amuse yourselves and live in sin, then you would be laying a shabby, shaky and sinking foundation because the Bible says that your sins shall find you out. Moses and Charlotte lived in sin during their courtship but did everything to hide it from the leaders. Finally, they got married and had a child. Their sin started haunting them and the marriage home became a rugged boat on a rough sea. The situation aggravated and both of them backslid from the faith. The next step was a divorce and soon after that, Charlotte died out of frustration. Today, Moses has left the faith and has even joined a satanic cult. May this not be your case in Jesus name! Take this time to fast and pray together for as many topics as possible. Praying together helps you to know one another physically, emotionally, and spiritually and thus develop ministry intimacy. It is however, advisable to pray in an open place like the church and preferably at daytime. The Bible advises us to give no opportunity to the devil because he would not spare. During our courtship, we practiced this, and two weeks before the wedding day, my fiancée and I took three days to fast and pray for the oncoming events and for our marital home. Thank God, we did it. We least suspected that the devil was cooking up a wicked plan to prevent us from getting married because he could foresee the hand of God on us. The legal marriage had taken place five months earlier and the devil had set us traps to fall in. Since we had resolved to keep the relation clean, the devil brought up another wicked plan. It was secretly arranged that the village chief should confiscate my wife since she was the female of a second set of twins to her mother. By tradition, she was supposed to be the chief's wife. So a ceremony was organized in the palace where the whole family was to show up and then she would be caught, rubbed with carmine traditional powder made from wood and then carried into the palace and that would sabotage all my marriage plans. Thank God for the spiritual preparation, God granted that the message should leak so she went into hiding and did not attend the ceremony. That day the chief and his notables did a thorough search but could not lay hands on her. All other previously unimagined upheavals came up until three days before the wedding ceremony, but our Lord was faithful to crush them all. Today we have been happily married for more than a quarter of a century. We celebrated our silver jubilee a few years back with great thanks to the Lord.

5. Study together

Many persons get into marriage ignorant of what it entails. Some discover their naivety only when problems start surfacing. Take the opportunity of the courtship period to read and interchange books on marriage and discuss some of the novelties in your findings. Caution is essential here about reading or discussing sexual matters. This is preferable after marriage. There is, however, a world of things to learn about marriage, adaptation, communication, resolving conflicts, keeping the home, parenting, planning ... the list is long. The learning process continues after marriage. Nowadays town Mayors who sign marriages in court are almost taking the place of pastors, preaching wonderful sermons, which often are not practiced by them. The Mayor who signed our wedding was one of those good orators and one thing I remember so well during his sermon is, "marriage is a school where you keep learning every day and never graduating. In fact you keep learning every day and even the day of your death, you would be learning how to die." Begin that process of learning while you are in courtship.

Dangers of the courtship period

As earlier said, though wonderful and fruitful as this courtship period can be, it is equally dangerous because it has to do with controlling emotions towards someone your heart goes out to and who is soon to be yours fully. It takes God's grace and self-control, an element of the fruit of the Holy Spirit to stay pure within and without until the wedding day. The dangers of lust and sexual sin are as real and as close as often as you meet. It is therefore of utmost importance to take every precaution necessary to flee away from the devil's trap. These are some guidelines.

1. **No late night visits:** Darkness gives power to sin manifestations. Night visits, dark and secret street corners, long moments in isolation are all risky grounds for the flesh to be aroused. Such moments must be avoided. In case of an obligatory night visit, it is necessary to be accompanied.

2. **Physical touch should be limited to the hands.** Apart from the sensual organs, there are many other body parts that are very sensitive and can arouse the sexual drive. The man should not allow the lady to caress his chest, abdomen or legs. In fact these body parts should not at all be exposed to her. The lady should **never** permit the hand of the young man to go over her breasts, lips, or into her dress. All these are provocative gestures that weep up sexual emotions. Mouth to mouth kissing, embracing and other forms of body contact are equally dangerous. Body contact should be limited to hand in glove as may be seen with persons taking a stroll. This may look very strict but prevention is better than cure. It is good to wait on the Lord for the appropriate timing.

3. **Special caution for the Ladies.** The ladies here should be more cautious when it comes to the sin problem because

there are better placed to help the men to resist temptation. There is a physiological difference between men and women when it comes to sexual arousal. Men are sexually aroused by sight. When a man sees a beautiful woman, with pointed breasts and rosy cheeks, and more so someone he loves, he can very easily be sexually aroused. But for women, they need to be caressed and fondled with alongside tender words of love. It is therefore important for the women to keep themselves from being touched carelessly by the male. The Bible says that your body is the temple of the Holy Spirit who lives in you. *Ladies you do not have to be that cheap and allow any hand on you anywhere and at any time. Keep preciously the temple of God and guard your future marriage from being damaged.* Do not forget that as it has often happened, the man could woo you to bed, use you and afterwards break the engagement. Please do everything to save your marriage.

Courtship is a desirous, wonderful and preparatory phase to a good marriage. When properly utilized by the fiancés, it becomes very rewarding in the future. It is also a delicate egg that needs to be protected from falling. If it does, it would break the marriage. You may still get married but your sins would haunt you. If you are in courtship already and have fallen, the best thing to do is not to hide your sin, but to see your pastor and open up to Him. God would give him the wisdom and discernment on how to handle your problem. The Bible says, 'He who convereth his sins shall not prosper, but whoso confesseth and forsakeh them shall have mercy' (Proverbs 28:13 KJV)

CHAPTER 12
After Marriage, What Next?

Before we get into the pleasures and pains of marital life it will be good to say something about the wedding ceremony. A wedding feast is an expensive ceremony that needs careful planning. In Western tradition, the bride's family takes care of the wedding bill; I experienced this when my adopted son married a white American. The man's family may just handle an evening collective dinner. In other continents, the two families may put their hands together to plan a budget. In Africa, it is different; the burden usually falls on the family of the bridegroom and very often on him alone. If there is no careful planning, the young man may find himself spending a lot of money only to fall bankrupt at the end of the ceremony. This is one of the causes of difficult times in some homes after marriage. It is therefore necessary to spend moderately for a wedding feast. In fact, my advice is that if you do not have money to make a feast, do not offer any. Marriage is not the feast but the union of two persons that have been blessed by God to begin a life together. Some people in an effort to protect their personality or social position go into debts because they want a loud wedding. They hence plunge themselves into debts that take months or years to pay.

My fiancée and I had agreed on a loud wedding with the aim of preaching the Gospel to all our invitees. We both hail from large backgrounds, aristocratic family personalities, and had invited personalities across the country. Our first evangelistic booklet entitled for that purpose, "A gift to you at our wedding" had been printed in several hundreds of copies with the same flowery background as the wedding cards. However, because of some reasons that I prefer not to mention here, we had to finance the party by ourselves from our meager savings. So we put in virtually all that we had and yet there were still unmet needs. There were some salary arrears in the tune of millions that we expected from the ministry of Finance, which we tried to obtain, in order to meet up the budget. We could not get the money before the wedding ceremony, which was God's will as it served us from financial disaster.

Good enough my wife was wise enough to keep aside some of the meat, chicken and foodstuffs that were being prepared for the wedding, otherwise we would have starved after the wedding. However, though the food was there, we were financially dry and had to wait for **o-n-e l-o-n-g m-o-n-t-h** before having any salary pay out. It was not easy to go along empty. God had to perform a miracle to see us through the period. As a business lady, my wife had hidden some time ago the **l-a-r-g-e** sum of fifty thousand francs in her valise. You understand the word **large** in context. So while we were organizing our things in the new house, we rediscovered this sum of money. You can imagine the praise and thanksgiving service that the two of us had in the house. This was manner from heaven to meet the needs of a young poor miserable couple who had squandered all their savings to feed a crowd.

The marriage feast is not the end of the matter. The door opens into a new life style. Be wise enough not to begin your marriage life by starving. Learn to plan and live according to your standards. That would be the beginning of wise planning.

The First Night

The marriage ceremony is a tedious and tiring ceremony and in some settings it usually continuous until late at night. The importance of a honeymoon hideaway is thus imperative. It is advisable to reserve a place away from your own home; a hotel room, a guest home or a room in the home of a close friend.

The first night is one of discovery but also one of embarrassment. It may be exciting for the faithful Christian Brother who has waited patiently through the courtship period, but for the sister, it is often embarrassing for her to have somebody suddenly step into her privacy and intimacy. It is not unusual for the sister to have an unexpected menstrual flow that day. This is a normal reaction to the stress of wedding preparation. When this happens, it is an extra test of patience. If he wants to fail the test then he could use preservatives, or the sister cleans up well before the first sexual contact.

Be careful not to rape your wife on the first night. Many sisters have complained that their husbands raped them at their first contact. This happens because the man is not patient enough, first to help the woman out of her psychological embarrassment, and then to adequately prepare her for the sexual act. Here again is a test of patience and love where the burning husband exercises self-retrain in order to prepare the woman sexually. We will not go into details about the sexual act because it is beyond the scope of this book. It is a chapter in our volume for the married entitled "The secret of a successful marriage."

Usually, with the excitement and embarrassment of that first night, both of you in conversation, gestures, or mannerism may make many mistakes. It is one of the moments that you start discovering the real person to whom you were hooked for life. Temperamental strengths and weaknesses begin to surface that first night. Each person must manifest an attitude of Christian maturity by being able to ask the other for forgiveness and to forgive in return.

Honeymoon

Because of financial constraints, many African couples never think of taking time away from friends, parents, relatives and their neighborhood to a quiet environment, or take a honeymoon trip where for some days, weeks, or even months they can just be by themselves. This is an important period because it permits them experiment some of the things they might have discussed during courtship. It permits them to know themselves practically; physically, emotionally and spiritually. Practical love and friendship becomes evident as the couple can freely enjoy one another's company, body and intimacy.

I had to counsel once a couple that had serious personality conflicts. They are a well to do couple with influential positions in society. They are a very busy couple who have great responsibility. In the course of our conversation, I realize that this couple never had a honeymoon. After marriage, they virtually went back to work and did not make time to know each other. Since then for the next seven years, they never had a weekend by themselves nor went away together for holidays. While his wife was breaking down under the pressure of job, housekeeping and parenting the children that came in succession, the husband was accusing her for not being the kind of gentle, submissive and loving wife he wanted. They have since not wanted to yield to counseling and the situation has worsen to that of a symbiotic relationship under the same roof. For several years, they have not slept in the same room. This is one of the consequences of not seeking to be together away from others.

Settling and getting to know one another
The weeks following marriage are a time of readjustment, learning and planning. There are many novelties to both individuals, which necessitates getting used to. Take for instance, before, the girl could stay for a day or two without bothering to cook, but now she has a husband to take care of and has no choice but to make meals for him. The husband may want to rest meanwhile his wife wants a drive and he has to go out of his way to accompany her. That is why the Bible says, "a married man is concerned about…how he can please the wife', *and* 'a married woman is concerned about…how she can please her husband' (1 Corinthians 7:32, 34).

Likewise, the man, who previously might have not bothered to come home immediately after work, has to rush home either because he loves the company of his darling wife or by marital obligation. Both of them may feel tired during the day because of few hours of sleep, but they still have to go about their daily duties. There are a couple of habits that need to be developed during this period to ensure a progressively succeeding marriage. They are communication, intimacy, on-going learning, transparency, and developing a forgiving spirit. We will look at the first two qualities here and the others in the last chapter.

a) **Communication:** Communication is one of the key elements to the success of a couple because it helps them to open to one another. While the men often know only one way of expression, which is verbal, the women are acquainted to other methods of communication that the men need to learn. These other methods include facial, touch and mannerism generally known as non-verbal communication. In marriage the woman loves to converse with her husband in order to get a feel of what he thinks, wants, or is imagining.

In verbal communication, she wants to know him more. You know the Bible says that it is out of the abundance of the heart that the mouth speaks. But usually the man would respond sharply to inquisitive questions by Yes or No. This is very frustrating to the one party who through those questions wanted to trigger a conversation. Often one of the parties does not really pay attention to the other. He may be answering questions while looking elsewhere or doing something else as if it were more important. This attitude is also discouraging. Women also like to communicate a lot with facial expressions - a wink of the eye, a sharp glance, or a piercing look. They expect their husbands to understand. In most cases, it is just a touch or a behavioral pattern that has an intrinsic meaning. Men who want to keep their home and build it must be ready to learn how to communicate in these various manners.

Lastly, some men and a few women have the habit of doing things without consulting or getting the consent, approval or opinion of their spouses. One party therefore finds itself faced with accomplished projects or programs, which may be of family interest but were single-handed. Communication dissipates any cloud of suspicion and establishes an atmosphere of confidence and mutual respect. Do not remain closed up. Open up to your spouse and your home will be a bed of roses.

b) **Intimacy:** This is another important aspect of the marital relationship. When we talk of intimacy, many people would immediately think of sexual relationship but that is far from it. Intimacy here relates to the expression of warm affections and admiration. Intimacy involves the interest that is reserved to one another, the level of commitment and friendliness. It includes the sharing of feelings, thoughts, affections, likes and dislikes. Lovers seek moments to be together, desire the company of one another and aspire for such times when they can confide in one another. They seek to please or protect the other and would do everything not to hurt one another. One's background, culture, educational level and even physical appearance or character could affect intimacy. However, where there is real love and a good dose of tolerance, intimacy helps to keep and strengthen the marriage relationship. The case of Franc and Melanie illustrate the absence of intimacy. Franc is from a polygamous background where his father hardly ever went out strolling with any of his wives. He is tall, quiet, and reserved. He enjoys reading, working, and being busy. On the other hand, Melanie is so short that her head hardly reaches his neck. She comes from a monogamous family where the family link was very warm. However, when she believed, the parents seriously molested her and finally threw her out of home in rejection. Since then she has been yearning for the man of her life who would fill in this emptiness with love and intimacy. She loves outings, adventure, company, and pleasure. They came to know each other in the university while studying in the same faculty. From the onset, Franc was driven towards Melanie by pity. He wanted to manifest concern to a solitary classmate, but their friendship gently grew into a love relationship. Despite the counselor's reservations about their relationship, they decided to get married. Not long after the forceful wedding ceremony, did the lack of intimacy become apparent. Franc in his reserved mood would prefer a quiet environment, would hardly engage a conversation, and would not satisfy Melanie with her numerous bugging questions. He would never think of going out with her, not even to have a ride with her in their old car. To Franc, the woman's place is at home and he can shuttle out from time to time to do important things. Melanie was dying for want of intimacy but unfortunately, she made the wrong choice. It is sad to say that despite their Christian convictions the marriage broke up because of these mark differences.

Marriage is a lifelong relationship – 'till death do us part'. It is therefore necessary not only to make the right choice but also to take time after marriage to nurture and build the relationship. I have always told those to whom I give premarital counseling and to the married that the bond of marriage is love. Where there is genuine love, there is a good marriage, but when this bond is hurt, disfigured or destroyed, marriage suffers. Every couple needs to know how to protect and keep strengthening this bond daily so that their marriage would be blissful. That is the object of the next chapter.

CHAPTER 13
Love: The Bond That Bides

The basis of marriage is love. It is the one thing that binds two persons together and should never be broken. As Dr. Warren says in his book, *Finding the love of your Life*, "Love is a highly complex process about which we know far too little. What we know is that without it, there are no great marriages." As we described in our first book destined to the married, *the Secret of a Successful Marriage*, there are different kinds of love when it concerns spouses. Companionship love, Compassionate love, Affectionate love, Romantic love and Passionate love are the five main types. Here, however, I just want to highlight the love procedure among lovers. When two persons fall in love, it usually starts with passionate love. That is why the expression "fall in love" comes about because it is an emotional drive accompanied by a strong desire to have the person for yourself and always. You would often hear statements like, "I have found the love of my life"; "I just feel great being by his/her side." There is such an irresistible inner yearning for the person. That is passionate love. The unfortunate thing is that often this great inner motivation does not remain for all time but may either gradually die down or stabilize. This kind of love propels those involved to indulge in fondling before marriage. Guilt and exposure to the privacy of one another destroys this passionate love. When marriage is contracted solely for this kind of love, it does not last because this kind of love may gradually fade after knowing each other sexually. Passionate love has to develop into companionship love. This is a more stable love dealing where the two develop a liking for one another's presence not just because of sex but also because of having found a true friend.

As Dr. Warren says, "compassionate love involves communication, commitment, caring, affection and support for one another." The Bible says that a friend loves at all times and sticks closer than a brother (Proverbs 17:17, 18:24). Companionship brings relief to one another. You have found someone who understands you, can listen to you and share your fears and joys, your most intimate and hidden feelings, and accept you just as you are. Your spouse is also someone, on whom you can pour out your reserve of intimacy, cares and concern without any complex. This is important because it is bilateral or reciprocal.

Companionship love has to develop into compassionate love. This is the level where commitment to one another is vital. Compassionate love includes the tenderness you show to the person during adverse circumstances, which may include physical or moral stress, sickness, hurts, tiredness and depression. It also involves financial responsibility towards your spouse and finally practical help.

Affectionate and romantic loves are very close to passionate love and need to be cultivated and built in marriage. They involve among other things sexual attraction, fondling with one another, caressing, and physical touch. The sad reality in many homes is that companionship and compassionate love is absent. You must be determined to give that to your spouse irrespective of the external and internal circumstances.

Once marriage has taken place, the question is no longer if you really love your spouse. One should rather concentrate on keeping the love bond and the marriage home healthy. Love expression in marriage must be constant, regular and renewable. Sentiments, affection, friendship, responsibility and commitment all describe this love expression. Let us study under three sub-heading characteristics of love in action in the marital home.

a) The love triangle

The Greek language has three different words for love but English bundles them all under the single word. The three Greek words are **Agape, Philio, and Eros**. In marriage, this three-dimensional love is necessary. Agape love talks of commitment to one another and involves our will or determination. Philio expresses the intimacy or camaraderie that is involved, and Eros talks of passion, emotions, or sexual expression. The Balswicks represent this diagrammatically in their book 'The Family' and this three-dimensional love finds expression in any family in one of four ways.

a) **A balanced marriage:** In a balanced marriage, the three kinds of love are represented thus,

Fig 13.1: Complete love

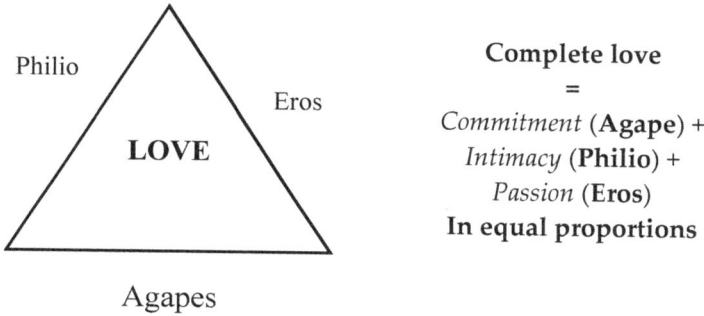

Philio

Eros

LOVE

Agapes

Complete love
=
Commitment (**Agape**) +
Intimacy (**Philio**) +
Passion (**Eros**)
In equal proportions

Commitment as discussed earlier is the time, concern, and care given to one another in marriage. It is the giving away of one's self for the other. Beside yourself you are often compelled by love to go out of your way, time, or pleasure to satisfy the other person. As the Bible puts it, 'a married man is concerned about...how he can please the wife', *and* 'a married woman is concerned about...how she can please her husband' (1 Corinthians 7: 32, 34).

Intimacy was treated in the previous chapter. Suffice to say here that it involves friendship of equal opportunities. Whether it is spending time together, sharing, going out for a stroll, or taking the other out for a pleasurable surprise there should be equal opportunities of it being expressed by both persons at different times. It should be pleasure for both persons. In a situation of true love, they enjoy the presence of one another and always look forward for such pleasurable moments.

Passion essentially refers to the sentimental side of marriage including verbal love expression, love play and the sexual act. Here it is traditional that the men that should trigger this aspect of love satisfaction as if the women do not have an erotic drive. It is, however, true that in any sexual act, the men will usually derive orgasm even if the woman does not, but it is normal that the woman should feel free to trigger the sexual act and help guide the husband to lead her to orgasm. It must however be understood by the men that the women often use nonverbal language to indicate their sexual desire, but the men are often too naive to understand it. More of this is explained in our book on *'secrets of a successful marriage'* in the chapter on the sexual act.

b) **Self-giving love:** This is the love relationship where the Agape love expression outweighs the other two. In such marriages, one party, usually the husband commits himself to satisfy the physical, financial, and social needs of the wife. The emotional need of intimacy and friendliness, and the erotic needs of passion, affection and sexual satisfaction are either neglected because of ignorance or much more often because of selfishness, lack of self-control, vengeance or as a punitive measure.

c) **Infatuation love**: In this kind of love defective relationship, the overriding element is sex. One or both persons are hyper-sexy and are regularly under the urge for a sexual act. They both enjoy it and are fulfilled one with the other as far as romance, affection, passion, and sex are concerned. However, the daily basic physical needs of one or the other may not be met, the neglected person may be dying of the need of intimacy and may be psychologically deprived, but the other does not sees, understand, or bother. What is important according to him/her is the bed. It could work well, at least for a time if the two are actively involved and enjoy sex, but when it is only a unilateral pressure, it quickly ends up in frustration, stress, bitterness, frigidity or one of the psychotic traumas. This kind of love expression is usually found among the newly wed who may be financially handicapped but enjoy all about sex.

d) **Friendship love:** The predominant factor is intimacy or camaraderie. They love one another's company and delight in sharing, staying together, outings, parties, and other outdoor manifestations. Socially, they are an exemplary couple but within, there is decay. One may be dissatisfied in bed and is getting emotionally upset, the other's needs are not being met and there is some dissatisfaction in the hearts and home. Outings and friendship may either be a cover up, the putting up of a face or a psychological inclination to compensate that, which is missing.

It may just be that the interest in sex has greatly diminished as in elderly couples, and they may not have much to live on, but they need the company of one another for survival. I visited such a couple several years back in the US. They were in their eighties and were alone in their apartment supporting each other in movement. At this age sex is not a vital need but mostly companionship and camaraderie. You could really see and sense that they loved each other.

b) Characteristics of love expression

If love is the engine of marriage, then communication is the oil that lubricates the engine. Forgiveness, and tolerance are the water that cools the engine and all these aspects are essential. We have already elaborated so much on communication; now let us see the other elements that characterize love expression in a martial relationship.

a) **Tolerance:** I deliberately decided to begin with this because it is the one element which when missing provokes many heartbreaks on both sides. On the one hand, the one needing to be accepted gets depressed and feels dejected. On the other hand, the one refusing to tolerate is enervated and begins to think that it was a wrong choice. Can you imagine two persons who have grown in different environments and circumstances to meet in a marriage home and suddenly blend? No matter the refine upbringing of one or both, they will always be flaws and I mean **always**. Spouses must be able to accept one another irrespective of weaknesses, disability, or failures. With time, patience, and re-adaptation, some of the unwanted characteristics may fade and the couple would tend to resemble one another both physically or in relation to character. Tolerance is an essential ingredient in the love soup bowl.

b) **Forgiveness:** Forgiveness in marriage is reciprocal. You must be ready to ask for forgiveness, to forgive or accept forgiveness. Some people do not know how to forgive themselves. Even when their spouse has forgiven them, they do not swallow the forgiveness but continue to blame themselves. We must be able to play this reciprocal game whether it is to our partner, children, or other members of the family.

c) **Learning:** Learning is a process that each family member must submit to. The husband is learning to know the wife and vice versa and the parents are learning to know the children and vice versa. There is no 'Mr. Know all' neither is it a master - student relationship. Each person is a master in one domain or the other and a student in another.

d) **Golden rule:** The golden rule of the Bible applies aptly in the marriage love relationship. Matthew 7:12 says, 'Do unto to others as you would have them do to you'.

The other elements including, care and concern for one another, communication, and open-heartedness as already established. I will end this section with two summarizing presentations, first a diagram and then secondly a quote from Saint Paul.

This diagram below summarizes our ideas about love expression in marriage.

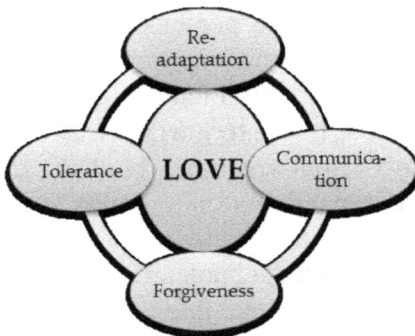

If LOVE is the engine of marriage, then communication is the oil that lubricates the engine and forgiveness and tolerance the water that cools the engine.

Re-adaptation is the key that ignites the process of learning, transformation and blending at every level and in every situation in order to make marriage a paradise on earth.

No other language can be more appropriate to express what love is all about than the words of Saint Paul addressed to the Corinthian church in the 13th chapter of his second book:

> *Love is patient, love is kind. It does not envy, it does not boast, it is not proud. It is not rude, it is not self-seeking, it is not easily angered, and it keeps no record of wrongs. Love does not delight in evil but rejoices with the truth. It always protects, always trusts, always hopes, and always perseveres. Love never fails.*

c) Love as a responsibility

The married home begins with two persons and gradually grows as children enter this nucleus. Love before marriage may be emotional and dreams but in marriage it is more than just emotional fulfillment and enjoyment, it is responsibility. It entails that the man handle his responsibilities, firstly, as lover, husband, breadwinner, and head of the home, and later, as father. The woman takes up duties as lover, helper, homemaker, and wife, and afterwards as mother. The role of children falls beyond the scope of this book.

As lover, husband, breadwinner, head of the home and father, the man assumes the following functions,

- Provides for the family's spiritual and physical needs, Genesis 3: 16-19; 1 Tim 5:8.
- Loves, protects and takes interest in the welfare of his wife and children, Ephesians 6:4.
- Honor, understand and appreciate his spouse, Col 3:19, 1Peter 3:7.
- Remain absolutely faithful to the marriage relationship, Mt 5:27-28.
- Represents the family in the society and defends its interests, Proverbs 31:23

His wife on her part has to submit to her husband, serve as helpmate in assisting him in household duties, grow into a homemaker, and assist the husband to teach the children God would bless them. Both spouses are to plan for the future of the family – spiritually, physically, materially, and financially.

Interdependence is the right word to describe the family relationship. The family is a web that binds together Father, Mother, Children and God. God should be in the center for everything to turn around Him as illustrated in the diagram below.

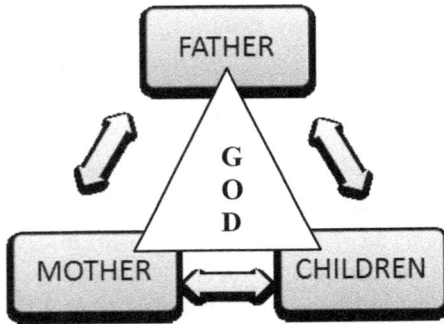

The sad reality is that many youths have thrown God out of their boy/girl relationship, courtship or marriage. The danger one runs in doing this is to live a life of infidelity, accompanied by guilt, shame and a gnawing complex. The greatest risk is that of having to spend eternity in the torments of hell where men will weep and gnash their teeth to no avail. Dear reader, permit me ask you a personal question. "Is your life right with God? Have you given your heart to Christ, or are you still swimming in the sea of sin?" The Bible says, "Do you not know that the wicked will not inherit the kingdom of God? Do not be deceived: Neither the sexually immoral nor idolaters nor adulterers nor male prostitutes nor homosexual offenders nor thieves nor the greedy nor drunkards nor slanderers nor swindlers will inherit the kingdom of God. That is what some of you were. But you were washed, you were sanctified, you were justified in the name of the Lord Jesus Christ and by the Spirit of our God" (1 Corinthians. 6:9-11).

This is the moment to make things right with your God. When the prodigal son did some introspection and saw his misery in loose living, he said to himself, " I will set out and go back to my father and say to him: Father, I have sinned against heaven and against you. I am no longer worthy to be called your son; make me like one of your hired men"(Luke 15:18-19). If you do not have a personal relationship with God it would be unfair to you and your future spouse to continue dabbling with sin, risking your future and eternity. You can accept Jesus Christ now as your personal Savior and Lord by opening your heart to him and praying this simple prayer or any other you can formulate.

> *Lord Jesus, thank you for loving me and opening my eyes to my sinful nature. I admit that I am a sinner and my life is not right before you. I have sinned in my thoughts, words and action. I believe that you died on the cross to set me free from all sin. Forgive me now and change the course of my life. Cleans me with your precious blood and purify me from all my iniquity. I accept you now as my Saviour and Lord. Come and live in me in the person of your Holy Spirit. Give me from this day victory over all sin and grant me self-control so that I can reserve myself hence for my future spouse. Lord I promise to live for you and to serve you for the rest of my life. Thank you Lord for saving me. AMEN.*

If you have given your life to Jesus through this book, start reading the Gospel of St John and contact us immediately for more help in your new life in Christ. Our address is at the end of the book.

CHAPTER 14
What Youths Need To Know About Sexually Transmitted Diseases (STDs)

What are STDs?

Sexually transmitted diseases are infections that contracted after a sexual relationship between an infected person and a healthy individual. Since one cannot identify a sexually infected person on the face, every sexual contact between two unmarried persons is always a potential danger. Because of the increasing promiscuity amongst youths and the unmarried, more than 250 million new cases of STDs are registered worldwide each year. Most of these diseases develop unnoticed but their long-term effects are devastating. In girls and women, they cause pelvic inflammatory diseases with lifelong pains, infertility, and ectopic pregnancies. Children born to such women may suffer eye infections and could even become blind. Men may develop infertility or chronic pelvic pains. Both sexes may die young because of advanced stages of syphilis. Most STDs if identified early can be treated, but it has been proven that these infections increase the chances of HIV/AIDS contamination as much as nine times. We obviously know that HIV/AIDS is the most virulent STD that till date has no curative treatment. God in warning us against sex out of marriage knew that it can destroy the immoral and adulterers.

STDs are caused by a variety of microorganisms including fungi, viruses, parasites, and bacteria. Many STDs develop without any symptoms and such people remain unconscious healthy carriers who share generously their germs with all their sexual partners. Therefore, the absence of symptoms or illness does not mean that one is free from a STD. Let us look at the most common STDs.

The most common STDs

1. AIDS: Today HIV/AIDS is the most commonly known and most dangerous sexually transmitted disease. It is dangerous in several ways. First, it is the greatest world pandemic that humanity has ever had and the number of infected persons keeps growing daily in millions. World statistics as of 2012[4] reveal the following

a) More than 34 million people now live with HIV/AIDS.
b) 3.3 million of them are under the age of 15.
c) In 2011, an estimated 2.5 million people were newly infected with HIV.
d) 330,000 were under the age of 15.
e) Every day nearly 7,000 people contract HIV—nearly 300 every hour.
f) In 2011, 1.7 million people died from AIDS.
g) 230,000 of them were under the age of 15.
h) Since the beginning of the epidemic, more than 60 million people have contracted HIV and nearly 30 million have died of HIV-related causes.

Africa South of the Sahara is the most affected place in the world. "More than two-thirds (69 per cent) of all people living with HIV, 23.5 million, live in sub-Saharan Africa—including 91 per cent of the world's HIV-positive children. In 2011, an estimated 1.8 million people in the region became newly infected. An estimated 1.2 million adults and children died of AIDS, accounting for 71 per cent of the world's AIDS deaths in 2011."[5]

From the statistics, it affects the sexually active age and thus the highest rates are found between 15 and 34-age range. The unfortunate truth is that up until today, there is no accepted curative treatment. All the medications used in its treatment are aimed at reducing the viral load in order to permit the seropositive live a normal life. Seropositive (HIV positive) cases are those that have the virus in their bodies but still look healthy and live like any other person. On the contrary, AIDS patients are those whose immune system has broken down to the point that they cannot more resist infections. They therefore manifest diverse kinds of infections. Symptoms would include

---

[4] http://www.amfar.org/about-hiv-and-aids/facts-and-stats/statistics--worldwide/ {Consulted 24th July 2013}
[5] http://www.amfar.org/about-hiv-and-aids/facts-and-stats/statistics--worldwide/ {Consulted 24th July 2013}

drastic weight loss, prolonged fever, chronic diarrhoea, lung infections including tuberculosis, fungi and viral body eruptions, and many other banal infections are all symptoms of the full-blown AIDS disease. God in His infinite wisdom proscribed sex for the unmarried because He knew it would be a source of destruction to them. Stay away from sexual immorality. The Bible even says, "Flee sexual immorality." The wise obey God.

i) Trichomoniasis, Candidiasis, or Bacteria vaginitis

These diseases mainly affect women though the men are not completely free. Trichomonas is a micro-parasite that causes a whitish foamy discharge while Candidiasis is a fungus that grows in the vaginal mucosa and causes a thick discharge causing perennial itching. Bacterial infections usually cause a yellowish purulent discharge. In men, Candidiasis causes red spots on the penis or urethritis. These infections cause a lot of discomfort in the woman and are treated with antibiotics but this has to be done only by competent medical services.

j) Gonorrhoea: Caused by the Neisseria gonococcus bacteria, it used to be the most common STD before the advent of AIDS. This disease can affect the genital organs, the throat, eyes and the rectum. It therefore can cause eye infection and blindness in new-born babies. This dangerous infection causes a lot of sterility in both women and men. The symptoms include painful micturition in men and women, a discharge at the tip of the penis and a vaginal discharge for the women. These symptoms however can pass unnoticed in the women while the disease continues its destructive pathway. That is what makes it a frequent cause of sterility in women. Proper medical treatment of sexual partners gives total cure but not permanent protection as the person can be re-infected as soon as he has a sexual contact with another carrier.

k) Syphilis: Syphilis is a vicious disease because it can develop insidiously. It is caused by the treponema pallidum and can be felt only one month after the contact. It causes a small wound called a soft chancre on the genitals and some swelling (ganglion) in the groins. The dreadful thing about syphilis is that its symptoms disappear after a few days while the disease continues to fester internally. If untreated it would result to a lot of devastating chronic problems including, skin, heart and nervous complications. Mother-child transmission during pregnancy results in intrauterine foetal death, malformation, or sick babies at birth. The Syphilis test is a compulsory test for all pregnant women in order to prevent foetal wasting.

l) **Chlamydia trachomatis:** is another dangerous disease that often develops insidiously in men and women. The woman may only notice the complications when the fallopian tubes are affected causing lower abdominal pains. Its discovery in the woman may be fortuitous or result from infertility. In the men however, it presents an abundant non-purulent discharge that turns to a clear viscous liquid.

m) **Pelvic Inflammatory disease (PID):** is a name given to all STDs that cause inflammation of the pelvis provoking great pains along with internal pelvic abscesses. Bacteria that climb through the genital tract affecting the uterus, fallopian tubes, ovaries and the soft tissue of the pelvis, cause PIDs. Gonorrhoea and Chlamydia are greatly incriminated. The inevitable complications include sterility and ectopic pregnancies resulting from the blockage of the fallopian tubes. Symptoms include fever, nausea, painful sexual intercourse, lower abdominal pains, spotting or heavy clotting during menstruation, and pains during micturition with unusual vaginal discharge. Proper treatment is required after some specific laboratory tests of the cervical and vaginal discharge.

n) **Genital Herpes:** A virus called herpes simplex causes it. After contact, the signs and symptoms appear between 2 and 20 days and are characterized by the appearance of a cluster of pimples on the genitals containing a clear fluid. These pimples are itchy and painful and when they burst, they form wounds and lesions on the genitals. All this could be accompanied by the appearance of Lymph nodes in the groins. In some cases, they are no real physical symptoms. In other cases, complications may result in infection and even death of the new-born. Another kind of herpes affects the lips and the eyes and is just as harmful.

Other STDs: Other STDs include:
♦   Hepatitis B that can be transmitted either through sex or by contact with the blood of an infected person,
♦   Phitiriasis caused by pubic louse,
♦   Scabies caused by Sarcoptes Scabeiei that dig under the skin creating furrows that provoke itching,
♦   Genitalia warts or Human Papilloma Virus (HPV) that produces warts of the genitals and could eventually develop into cancer,
♦   Chancroid caused by a bacteria called Haemophylus ducreyi producing small pimples and ulcers on the genitalia and often swollen lymph nodes and fever, and
♦   Cytomegalovirus (CMV) which causes malformations in babies.

STDs and YOU
You do not have to suffer at all from any of these STDs. Every STD results from sin, though some people may contact these diseases otherwise. This is the case of new-borns with AIDS, Syphilis or Gonococcal eye infections. Some people may also contact AIDS and Hepatitis through either blood transfusion or contamination with infected blood. As we already said before all sexual acts out of marriage is sin whether it is among youths – fornication, or involving the married – adultery. Today, there are many more manifestations of sexual immorality including, lust, homosexuality, pornography, paedophilia and zoophilia as already mentioned in a preceding chapter. The Bible says, *"Flee from sexual immorality. All other sins a man commits are outside his body, but he who sins sexually sins against his own body" (1 Corinthians 6:18).*
If you had sexual activity before believing, I advise you to consult a Medical Doctor for a good check-up so that if you

are a healthy carrier of any of the STDs mentioned above, you would benefit from proper treatment before ever getting married. This is important because you could carry an infection into your marital home and not only contaminate your spouse, but endanger the whole family by creating unnecessary heartaches. If you are still a natural virgin, I congratulate you and emphasize that you keep to your vow of virginity until you get married. May God grant you His grace to stand firm.

CHAPTER 15
Questions and Answers on Sex and the Adolescents

Through our numerous singles seminars, we have been asked several interesting questions. We have selected some of the most pertinent ones that can actually help more youths in decision-making.

Question 1: *How can one foresee the first experience of a wet dream or menstrual flow in order to prepare for it? What should I do when it occurs?*

Answer: It is quite difficult to foresee the date of your first menstrual flow or wet dream. However, when a young girl of about nine, starts developing breasts, pubic and axially hair, she should be ready that the menses could come any time. Maternal counseling at this time is very important. Usually the menses may come at a moment you least expected - in class, in a crowd, car or some other social gathering. There should be no panic or shame. If it were overt, most of the adults there would understand. It may be advisable, prior to this, to always go around with some toilet paper, cotton or pads in your handbag. For boys, it is absolutely no problem because wet dreams occur usually at night and the boy may realize only in the morning that his pant is wet. Paternal counseling during this period is also vital.

Question 2: *If you do not see your menses regularly does that mean that you are sick or pregnant? What should you do if you have not seen your menses?*

Answer: Menstrual flow takes place every month. Usually the uterine lining prepares for pregnancy every month. If there is none, the uterine lining breaks down and flows out as menses. For 2 to 5 days, the woman bleeds. When a girl with a regular monthly flow does not see her menses in a given month, the chances are that she is pregnant. This is almost certain if she had a sexual intercourse within that period. But for some adolescents, who have just started having menses, the physiological changes are not fully established and from time to time the girl may miss her menses or have a delayed flow. This is normal and there should be no panic. However, if this continues for several months then it would be better to consult a Medical Doctor for proper diagnosis.

Question 3: *Why is it that at the age of 13 and above many girls begin to examine their intimate parts?*
Answer: This may be more common with the girls, but it happens to both sexes and the reason is obvious. There are a lot of physiological changes and these youths start becoming conscious of their femininity or masculinity. Because the breast and pubic hair are developing in the girls accompanied by a monthly menstrual flow, they become curious to understand what is happening. For the boys, the changes in the voice, the growth of body hair and the increase in size of the penis also make him interested in observing these body parts. Lastly, the sexual emotion is on and difficult to handle. At times fondling with these organs gives some pleasure but this attitude may result in masturbation. One has to be careful not to fall in the sin of masturbation, lust or fornication.

Question 4: *What is masturbation and how can one avoid it?*
Answer: Masturbation is the act of stimulating one's sexual organs by hands or some other method without sexual contact. The purpose is to derive some sexual satisfaction. It usually occurs in the both sexes when they are sexually excited. It is a dirty habit because it can introduce germs in your sexual organs and cause an infection. It is also a sin before God because it is a manifestation of lack of self-control. There are three things you can do to prevent or stop masturbation and any other sexual sin. First of all, avoid all that arouses sexual desires. **Stop** reading romantic novels, watching sexy or romantic films. Girls should not at all allow boys to touch them or play carelessly with them. Boys on their part should not frequent environments where girls are sexily dressed. The Bible says, *"Each one is tempted when, by his own desires, he is dragged away and enticed. Then, after desire has conceived, it gives birth to sin; and sin, when it is*

full-grown, gives birth to death" (James 1:14-15). Secondly, ask God to renew your mind and give you the ability to control your sexual emotions (Romans 12:2). This is because masturbation is first nursed in the mind before it is practiced. Lastly, flee from all appearance of sexual sin. Learn to set your mind on heavenly things, especially praise when you have sexual desires. Also seek the company of another Christian of the same sex so that both of you can share and pray together.

Question 5: *During what period of the month do youths have a sexual drive and what do you do to control it?*
Answer: The boys have no particular timing. For a week or two, boys may have a strong sexual urge. After that they could go for several months, before having another such trying period. This is a dangerous period for them because they can fall in sin. For girls, it usually comes up once a month and that is in the middle of their menstrual cycle - during the fertile days. The fertile period is the period during which a girl can become pregnant if she has sexual contact. It starts two days before ovulation (the release of the ovum or egg) and continues for two or three days after ovulation. The girl's sex organs prepare for sexual intercourse and fertilization of the released ovum. Her body therefore renders all favorable conditions for sex. She develops a strong sexual drive towards boys, her vagina secrets slimy mucous to prepare for a sexual relation and girls can easily fall into sin then. During this moment some girls easily give in for a sexual relation and get pregnant without knowing. It is normal and natural to have a sexual drive. Ask God for grace and self-control. The Holy Spirit will grant you victory over these trying moments.

Questions 6: *Is it true that as a young person it is unhealthy to stay without sex?*
Answer: Some youths during our seminars have said that medical doctors told them that they couldn't stay without sex because it is not healthy. This is a pure lie of the devil. If a doctor dares say a thing like that to a girl, that girl should be careful because he may want to take her to bed. God, who

created our bodies and knows best how they function, says that every sexual act committed before marriage is a grievous sin. In fact, in the Bible fornication or adultery was punishable by death (Deuteronomy 22:13-28). You remember that a woman was brought to Jesus to be stoned to death according to the law because she was caught in adultery (John 8:4-11). Jesus forgave her and asked her to stop living in her sin. If people were still being stoned today because of the sexual sin, would you still be alive? Jesus wants to forgive you and give you power to live a holy life for Him. He also wants to tell you, "I forgive you all your sins. Go and sin no more."

Question 7: *Why do some youths become disobedient to their parents during this period of puberty?*
Answer: Adolescents are neither children nor adults. They are in the process of becoming adults. It is a transitional stage. But many of them begin to feel and think that they are adults on the same footing with their parents. They begin to think that their parents are exercising too much control over them, whereas they need their liberty. They think they are responsible. Disobedience at this period also has to do with temperamental type and upbringing. It could also be a reaction to guilt after falling in the sexual sin. Parents should watch over their adolescent children and pray for them earnestly. Youths need their parents most during this period. It is not time to treat them like children but to dialogue with them and counsel them because sin is knocking at their door through a new opening called sexual instincts. Christian children at this time should show signs of good upbringing by being submissive to their God- fearing parents. The Bible says, "Children, obey your parents in the Lord, for this is right. Honor your father and mother – which is the first commandment with a promise – that it may go well with you and that you may enjoy long life on the earth" (Ephesians 6:1-3).

Question 8: *If you have fallen in the sexual sin, if a man or girl has forced you to bed, what should you do? Suppose you were* *already given to it before believing, now as a child of God how can you resist what you are already used to?*

Answer: Here, we are dealing with two conditions. The first case is that of a youth who has been raped or forced to bed by someone of the opposite sex. This is a serious problem because it affects you psychologically and physically. I heard the testimony of a girl who was forced to bed by her teacher and this affected her terribly for several years. Though a bright student, she could no longer pass her examinations. She was demoralized and psychologically traumatized. The first advice here is to warn you from getting too close to people of the opposite sex. Even if a man is as old as your father, it is no guarantee that he cannot be tempted to take you to bed. If you have already fallen, repent and immediately seek counseling from a real born again Pastor.

The second case is that of someone who is or was already involved in the sexual sin. The Bible is very strict against this sin. *"Flee from sexual immorality. All other sins a man commits are outside his body, but he who sins sexually sins against his own body. Do you not know that your body is a temple of the Holy Spirit, who is in you, whom you have received from God? You are not your own; you were bought at a price. Therefore honour God with your body."(1 Corinthians 6:19-20)* There is no habit that cannot be broken. If you are serious with your spiritual life cut physical links with **all your previous sexual partners.** Let them know that you have become a child of God. Pray and ask God to deliver you from lust and immoral thoughts. Ask Him to renew your mind and give you victory over all sexual temptations. You also need to open up to a man of God for counseling and prayers.

Question 9: *Is there anything wrong with having a boy or girl friend. Don't you need one as an adolescent?*

Answer: There is absolutely nothing wrong with having boy or girl friends if your motives are pure. But let me ask you a simple question. What do you need a boy or girl friend for? The Bible says that bad company corrupts good morals (1 Corinthians 15: 58). If you have bad friends, they would help you to sin but if your friends are **committed** believers, they **could** help you spiritually. I have highlighted 'committed' and 'could' because even believers can get you to sin. The Bible says that those who stand take heed less they fall. *As an adolescent you do not need an intimate friend of the opposite sex. It is not necessary. It will only whip up your sexual emotions to sin.* So long as you belong to a youth group where you can interact with your age mates of both sexes, that is enough. Boy and girl friend relationship for a teenager is a trap of Satan to plunge you into sin and make you a slave to your emotions. Do not fall in the trap.

Question 10: *Are itches and vaginal discharges a sign of disease?*
Answer: Itches around the perineum for both sexes are a sign of fungi infection or some other disease. It is not good to do self-medication because you can complicate the infection. It is good to consult immediately. As for vaginal discharge it is different. There is a kind of a vaginal discharge that is normal. This kind is whitish, not foul adored, not abundant and not uncomfortable. But when a discharge is thick like milk clots, or foamy like soap bubbles, if it is yellowish or foul smelling and is abundant, making you uncomfortable, then it is infectious and the person should consult a Medical officer immediately.

Question 11: *Why is the topic of sex a taboo in our society? Can it not become a topic for moral instruction in schools?*
Answer: In the past, parents would not want their children to know about sex because they were afraid they would venture forbidden territories. But today, knowledge of sex can be found everywhere; in television programs, in books, internet, and in discussions among peers. Children, who then are not advised by their parents, receive wrong counseling from friends, books, the media and from websites and fall prey to wrong sexual habits, including kissing, caressing, masturbation, fornication, adultery and even homosexuality. Today, our youths are a high risk group not only because of these sinful practices, but also because of the risk of contracting the deadly yet incurable

142

disease AIDS. It is of great importance today that parents should carry out sex education. It is also necessary for sex education to be carried out in Christian youth gatherings and schools. It must be emphasized that committed Christians should do it otherwise their silence could have negative repercussions on their youths. By reading this book, you have received some sex education. If you have more questions on the topic, or things you do not yet understand, ask for more from your parents at home or your Pastor. My payer for you is that God will establish you in purity and that you will keep your virginity until your marriage day. May God richly bless you as you hold firm on your vow of virginity.

CHAPTER 16
Questions and Answers on Marriage

We cannot exhaust the series of questions asked by youths on marriage during our seminars. Below are answers to some we deem pertinent. We advise the unmarried to ask all remaining questions to their parents or spiritual leaders.

Q 1: *Is there anything wrong if a girl gets married to a boy who is younger than her? Is it against Bible teaching since many people say that Adam was created before Eve?*

Answer: Marriage is based on **love** and not on age. It is however necessary to consider the age factor because women age faster than men. A man who wants to get married to a girl much older than him must consider the fact that she may age much faster than he thought. I have often made the mistake of asking some husbands if the wife they brought for consultation was their mother. The next point to consider is that of submission. If there is genuine love, even an older girl would be ready to submit to her husband. Lastly, be careful you do not want to get married to someone younger or older than you out of external pressure, frustration or financial benefits. It must be out of genuine love.

Q 2: *If I get married to an unbeliever, is that wrong? There are cases where a girl or boy got affianced to an unbeliever before accepting Christ. In that case can they not continue with the relation and get married even when one party is still an unbeliever? After all, they genuinely love themselves.*

Answer: The passage of 2 Corinthians 6: 14-17 is a very clear answer to this question. It is better to break an engagement than to break a marriage. Even if some financial expenditure has taken place, it can be refunded. Remember that none of us can bring someone to the Lord. The Holy Spirit convicts. Getting into such a marriage would be like boarding a plane you are not sure would reach its destination because it has some mechanical or electronic faults. The decision is yours and the consequences also.

Q 3: *Which are the best and worst temperamental marriage combinations? How do I choose the temperament I should get married to?*

Answer: We do not get married to a temperament but to a person. There is nobody with only one temperament. Everyone is a combination of different temperaments in varying degrees. No one temperament is better than another. No matter one's temperament, it can be positively influenced by the Holy Spirit if the person is submissive. However, it is good to be careful not to have two explosive characters together. If two dominant personalities get married, each with an iron will or explosive anger, they can set their marriage on fire. On the other hand, if a Steady personality gets married to another one, family issues may go unattended to because of their sluggishness. It is just good to pray and study the character of the one you love to make sure that you are a good blend.

Q 4: *Can a sister not get married to a jobless brother and take care of him? Can the sister not be the bread winner?*

Answer: The Bible says that he who does not work should also not eat and that he who cannot provide for his family is worse than an infidel. It depends on what we mean by joblessness. I am a Medical Doctor by training. If I cannot have a medical job I would be jobless but that does not prevent me from doing some farm work, open up a store or do some other small business that can earn me some money. In reality, when we talk of joblessness it simply implies that the person is not industrious, creative or humble enough to do menial jobs. The Bible says clearly that the man is the breadwinner of the family. He must show signs of this even if the wife will support in a greater way.

Q 5: *Can we get married against the will of our parents? Must they agree before our marriage?*

Answer: This issue of parental consent is mainly African. In America and Europe, parents have no big role in the final decision. However, as much as possible, let us get our parents' approval. There may be a few extreme cases where this may not be possible. In such cases, it would be important to confer with your spiritual leaders before taking any decision.

Q 6: *Can a sister in love with a brother not move up to him to propose? What is wrong with that?*
Answer: I do not see any biblical example. In that case who is marrying the other? Are you the one taking him into marriage or the reverse? Remember the Bible says the man is the one who takes a woman for a wife. Doesn't nature itself show that the woman is graceful and more reserved? I would advise that if a girl falls in love with a boy, instead of going to propose, let her fast and pray that God will touch the young man's heart. She can also use genuine nonverbal ways to show she is in love but let the proposal be the man's affair. I think this is the biblical pattern.

Q 7: *Why should one expose one's past life to the person one is planning to marry when God has forgiven you and forgotten? Is that not a way of resurfacing old wounds?*
Answer: That is quite right. But we also often remember these things when we are praising and worshipping God for what He has done in our lives. When we talk of these things it is not just because we want to unbury the past, it is because we want our future spouse to know who we are and where we have been. It must be understood that our past, influences our future, and that is why knowing what our past has been can help us to positively modify our future. If keeping a record of the past were not important, history would be uncalled for. If it exists then we should also keep and share our past with those that are dear to us.

Q 8: *If someone sponsored you in school, disvirgined you or has a child with you, is that not reason enough to marry the person when there is still burning love? If not how do you come out of the situation?*
Answer: This question is similar to Q 2. History has proved that many of such marriages do not work because something

else is at the basis of the relationship. It is either the financial expenditure, the attachment because he disvirgined you or the child that resulted from your life of immorality. Spare yourself the trauma of a future divorce when all these collateral would have faded. If you are honest to find out if God is in your relationship, your answer would be obvious.

Q 9: *Now that AIDS has become very rampant, from your standpoint are you saying that there is no marriage for AIDS carriers? Would that be the same case for Sickle cell patients?*

Answer: This is an important question because there are many believers today who are seropositive or with the AIDS disease and we have to consider them with love. I will not advice a marriage between an AIDS patient and a healthy person, but will accept marriage in two cases. First of all between a non-infected person and a well-controlled seropositive who is following his/her treatment regularly and is under medical surveillance; secondly between two seropositive. They would be advised to use preservatives during sexual contact in order to avoid exchange of viral strains. Child bearing would therefore be studied carefully for such couples. It is however, known today that seropositive women who are on regular treatment would not pass the infection to their pregnancy. They would however, need medical counseling and follow-up.

Concerning the Sickle cell disease, a homozygote Sickle cell patient (SS) can get married to someone with normal haemoglobin. Their children would be carriers without suffering from the disease. However, it must be understood that women with this disease have difficult pregnancies.

Q 10: *If there is genuine love amongst two persons and they are sure of God's will but their leaders' say it is not God's will, what should they do?*

Answer: This is a difficult situation but not impossible. I have two testimonies to this effect. In the first case, the two persons went elsewhere and looked for a pastor who wedded them. The marriage went on for a couple of years and they had two children amidst rising conflicts. Finally, the marriage could not stand and today they are divorced and thousands of miles apart. In the second case, the two people got married and their marriage apparently is going on well. What I am saying is that one of the parties must be wrong, either the leaders or more likely those in love. I would advise that the two persons should be patient and go back to prayer until God either convinces the leaders or disapproves of the relationship. It is better to wait for God's clarification than to jump into a relation that would destroy you in future. It may be good also to consult the opinion of a neutral spiritual leader.

Q 11: *You give us the impression that making a choice for a life partner is a difficult thing. Are you also saying that marriage is a heart-breaking relationship?*

Answer: Marriage is an institution ordained by God and all that He created is wonderful when used according to His norms. The Bible says that he who finds a wife finds a good thing and gains a favor from the Lord. Marriage is sweet and desirable. But anything that is important and precious must be worked for and taken care of. I have often said in our seminars that there are three important decisions in life for any person. The first and most important is the decision to accept Christ as your Savior. I hope you have done so. If not turn to the last page of this book and make that commitment. The second is the choice of a life career. People are better at specific jobs depending on their temperaments and attractions. The last decision is that of the choice of a life partner. That is what this book is all about. Preserve your virginity. Fast and pray as you seek the face of God for the right life partner. If you get into the wrong marriage, it will be most unfortunate for you because you will be in for a lifetime of regret, difficulties and frustration. It could even cause you to backslide and lose your salvation. However, if you make the right choice by God's grace, you would begin a life of enjoyment and fruitfulness in all areas of life. If you want a beautiful marriage, you have to prepare for it. I would like to pray with and for you:

"Lord Jesus, I present to you this day your dear son/daughter. You have ordained a future for him/her and I pray that your perfect plan for his/her life will be accomplished in JESUS NAME. As he/she has committed his/her life to seek your face and your perfect will, I pray that it will come to pass for your glory. I pray Lord that from this day you will grant her/him victory over all sexual temptations and grant him/her to keep the virginity vow in JESUS NAME. Through him/her Lord I pray that you will add another successful marriage that will cause destruction in the devil's kingdom and bring glory to your name. Lord I pray that from this day onward you will preserve and protect his/her testimony and guide him/her to the right choice of a life partner in JESUS NAME. I pray the blessings of the Lord upon you now in JESUS NAME. Blessings of protection, commitment, guidance, prosperity and victory be yours from today onward. Lord, I pray that all those who pray and believe this prayer will equally receive all divine favours from you in the glorious name of our LORD and SAVIOUR JESUS CHRIST. Amen."

Bibliography and Suggested Reading

Daniel Shu; **The secret of a successful marriage**. Vita press B. P. 11365 Yaounde Cameroon. 2000

Jack O. Balswich and Judith Balswich; **The Family, a Christian perspective on the contemporary home.** Baker book House Grand Rapids, Michigan 49516

La Haye Tim; **Spirit controlled temperaments.** Eastbourne; Kingsway publication LTD, P.O. Box 827, BN 21 3YJ, 1997

Lee Ellis and Larry Burkett; **Your Career in changing times.** Chicago; Moody Press. 1977

Neil Clark Warren; **Finding the love of your life.** Tyndale home publishers, Wheaton, Illinois 1992

William J. Petersen; **Martin Luther had a wife.** Bridge publishing, Chepstow Gwent (UK) 1984

Order from

LEAD Library
Yaounde Cameroon
Email: drdanielshu@yahoo.com
Tel: 00237 7898 9771
www.lucidedu.org

Our contact address is

Dr Daniel SHU
P.O. BOX 35166 Bastos Yaounde
CAMEROON, AFRICA
Tel: +237 7761 2598
drdanielshu@yahoo.com
www.lucidedu.org

www.ingramcontent.com/pod-product-compliance
Lightning Source LLC
Chambersburg PA
CBHW030653270326
41929CB00007B/348